A LIFE UNFOLDING
GROWING UP IN WALES IN THE
50's, 60's, AND 70's

Howard Westcott

Published by New Generation Publishing in 2021

Paperback: 978-1-80369-010-0
Hardback: 978-1-80369-011-7
Ebook: 978-1-80369-012-4

www.newgeneration-publishing.com

New Generation Publishing

ACKNOWLEGEMENTS AND PROLOGUE

This book is over 30 years in the making. I always wanted to write it. It was not about anyone special, which I am not, but to look at growing up in the South Wales Valleys and then my time in Cardiff through my eyes. There are many who were born and brought up in Wales and have since moved to all corners of the globe, nostalgia is a powerful emotion and I tried to trigger those feelings. This time however was not just about the Valleys and Cardiff but how I saw the world in general.

The 60's and 70's were a period of great change, from the post war 50's and the aftermath of World War 2, which took some time to recover from, then through the massive realignment in the 60's which I was swept up in. A growing pop culture where music, attitudes and acceptance of the strict rules of society were beginning to be questioned, mainly by the younger generation, of which I was part. The horrors of racism and bigotry were loudly questioned and demonstrated against, The assassinations of JFK, and later in the decade, Martin Luther King, the further horrors of apartheid in South Africa, Woodstock, the Stones, Beatles, Dylan taking over from the sanitized 'pop culture of the early 60's. During that decade add the Cuban Missile Crisis of 1962. I was only 10 then but learnt more about it as the decade went on, with the world teetering on war and the standoff between Kennedy and Khrushchev. Then later in the 60's the Russian Invasion of Czechoslovakia in 1968 when I was now 16 and I was concerned in what was happening in the world around me. The crushing of the liberalization instigated by a brave man, Alexander Dubcek was appalling to me. Adding to the beginnings of the 70's with Watergate, the despots of Africa, including one of the worst of all, Idi Amin, and the influx of Ugandan refugees into the UK. The other African event which had a long-term effect on me was the Nigerian Civil War of 1967 to 1970, better known as the Biafran crisis and the images in 1968 of malnourished children literally dying where they stood in their thousands shown on the TV shocked and horrified me. It was brought back again in the early 80's with Michael Burke's harrowing documentary on the situation in Ethiopia, which to me was the Biafran crisis all over again. Then came Live Aid and more sophisticated communications which no doubt did improve the situation. I was no lover of Bob Geldof before, but his bloody minded desire to do something practical is to be admired, well it was to me.

Also the Iron fist of Russia was to dominate my early years. It wasn't until the fall of the Berlin Wall in the late 80's that the Iron fist started to loosen, and the old USSR became Russia, but that was a while away . Remember also that Homosexual activity amongst men was illegal until 1967, and even then it only applied to 2 males in private over the age of 21, it was 1994 before it was reduced to 18 and as late as 2000 before it was reduced to 16. The whole area of LGBT legislation took even longer , and it would be naïve to believe that hostility in this area has been eliminated, but progress has been made.

So in my 60's and 70's world, 'The times they were a changin'. I was in the middle of this heady mix and this was the backdrop of my world which I grew up in and undoubtedly it had an effect on who I was and what I became. I am so glad in many ways I went the route I did and have fought intolerance and discrimination of all forms all my life, and will continue to do so until I take my last breath.

The book is a series of short stories, sometimes chronological and some not. I tried to express a range of emotions, that we all went through, happiness, sadness, tears, laughter and the many mistakes we all make, thrown into the melting pot which makes us who we are. And then you realize life for all of us is just a series of what if's.

You will meet Walt, Teo, Alun, Rita, Rosie and last but certainly not least Lily. I hope you can relate to them as much as I did.

I started to write this again about 4 years ago, but just put it away, until I decided as I am getting older to do it. I am just finishing my teaching career and thought that now is the time.

Without my wife and best friend of nearly 20 years, Suzy, I probably would not have done it, she encouraged me to do it and supported me through the whole process, checking spelling, continuity etc and reading it as someone who had bought the book and was looking at it from a readers point of view.

My Sister Helen, who still lives in the Cardiff area, although she is 6 years younger than me, was part of this time She is also the family historian and provided dates and pictures of that time, plus she was 'Head of Research'!!

Dave Patterson, who is a Cardiff man, read many chapters for his view on my perceptions of Cardiff at that time to check accuracy.

The photos in this book, only come mainly from 2 sources, the pre-Cardiff Pictures come from the family collection. The Cardiff pictures come from a great photographer called Tony Othen who gave me written permission to use some of his very emotive pictures of Cardiff in the 1970's. Thank you Tony.

The front cover is a carved oak statue called 'Keeper of the Collieries'. It was carved above the Llynfi Valley by a talented Welsh artist, Chris Wood, who kindly gave me permission to use it. The statue is 9 foot tall and has become an iconic image of those tough times and people, throughout the South Wales Valleys. Chris informed me the statue was based on an old miner called Bill Richings. I suggest that you look at Chris's other carvings via his website www.woodartworks.co.uk. Many thanks Chris.

In some of the tales the names are fictitious but the events did happen.

Don't think I have forgotten anybody, (but probably have!!) and I hope you enjoy this.

Howard

Contents

CHAPTER 1

THE EARLY DAYS

I have decided to put this into words now as I get older, it is not some form of therapy (perhaps it is?) but I am trying to find out why I am the person I am now, and what my background meant to me. If you are looking for raunchy sex scenes and language then put the book away. As you will see there were periods where perhaps some of these things happened, but it is just part of my jigsaw. This book is about me, growing up in the 50's, 60's and 70's, looking at the world through my eyes, if in others it strikes a note or two then I am even happier....

My name is Howard, yes ordinary and says nothing, not exotic or creating an image of some form of exciting upbringing, but this was the South Wales valleys in the 1950's, my surname was at least not Jones, Thomas or Davies, but Westcott. My middle name is John, I wanted more mystique even for a middle name, my dad was into the big bands of the 30's and 40's, Glenn Miller, Tommy Dorsey. How I would have liked Howard Glenn? , Count Basie? Cab Calloway? Duke Ellington?, My dad loved them all, I remember Spike Jones and his City Slickers, Howard Spike Westcott...better. Howard Count Duke Westcott, a little over the top I feel. But Howard John it was. If I am going to put this book together then it is important to me to see how my early life growing up affected me as an adult. So I will give you some background of my family which can help put my life in some sort of context.

I was born in the July of 1952 in Neath. The first born of my parents Mary and Gordon, my sister Helen followed 6 years later. Dad was a local bobby. The very early days I do not remember, we lived in a little village called Croeserw for nearly 5 years of which I have no recollection, only through some old family photos. My memory starts to kick in when we moved to a village called Glyncorrwg, close to Maesteg. In those days it's only claim to fame was it had the highest rainfall in Great Britain. It was a one road in, one road out place, surrounded by high mountains either side in front of you. I went to school there of which I have vague memories, but the jewel in the crown was the local post office/ general store/ sweet shop which was run by one of my aunts and uncles, Dolly and Joe.

My mum was 1 of 6 children, 4 daughters and 2 sons, all 4 daughters were close, most of them lived and stayed in the Maesteg area their whole lives. They all married, but unusually my mum was the only one to marry a Welshman. Ivy who lived in Maesteg and looked after my grandfather, married a Scot, Richard. Dolly and Betty married men from the North of England, Joe and Bill, who both moved down to Wales.

My sister filled in some background of my family which I was not aware of which I will share with you. My grandfather on my mother's side John Williams, lived in Maesteg most of his life. At about 14/15 he was down the mines as a hewer and miner, same as his grandfather, William Williams, before him who did the same jobs in the mines, his father died early. My maternal grandmother died in 1946 and there is only one known picture in existence which is included in this book. Maesteg in those early days had 4 mines, an iron works and tin works, not as big by a long way as the Merthyr story I relate in a later chapter, and much of this coal and ore went to Porthcawl which eventually had a railway and dock but it was short lived, and was nowhere near the size of Swansea, Cardiff or Newport. It was a classic ' How Green was my Valley' lifestyle, 9 in a small 2 up and 2 down house, no inside toilet, no money and a difficult life. Until the end of his life he was a Welsh speaker first. My sister took photographs for me in the Valleys where we were brought up, one is the back cover of this book and a few inside. The front cover is a fantastic carved 9 foot oak statue above Maesteg called 'The Keeper of the Colliery' overlooking and representing the mining, iron and tin industries that were the bedrock of these communities. Both my sister and I are proud to be from that mining background, which until the research for this book, I was not aware of. We think we have it tough, how they brought up 6 children in a tiny house to be the good people they all were is a testament to them and the reason the daughters especially, cared for their father till his dying day.

My father came from a different background, his family were from farming and nursing stock. An older relative, Lieutenant Colonel George Westcott OBE JP, was a Lord Mayor of Manchester in 1928/9 and an influential figure in the day . His son, John Shorland Westcott, was a renowned architect and spent most of his career in Lagos Nigeria, where he is buried. He died quite young at 40, after a flying accident in Lagos. He also had a distinguished war career in the Royal Engineers. His picture is a spitting image of my Dad at the same age plus he was a good rugby player and played for Wilmslow in Manchester, where the family rugby link seemed to begin. Your family does shape the person who you become, two of that generation went to the USA and my sister has tracked down that link as well..

More direct links are, my grandfather on my father's side (Dad's Dad) was Thomas George Westcott, the great grandfather was also a Thomas Westcott and my father's middle name was also Thomas, Gordon Thomas Westcott, but it was not passed down to me. I would not have minded if it was. In fact I would have preferred Howard Thomas Westcott than Howard John. The older generation hailed from farming backgrounds in Devon. Some pictures show my grandad with my dad, me and my sister in one of the caravans in Porthcawl with him, who we called Pops. The facial resemblances are there and now I am older I bear a close resemblance to my Dad. I am happy with that.

Anyway back to Glyncorrwg, the highlight of my week was going to the shop to see my aunt and uncle and going behind the counter. It was like Aladdin's cave to us. I must have been 8 or 9 by now and my sister 3. I recall the smell and excitement of going in there. It was typical of all the Valleys at that time, but especially Glyncorrwg, where everybody knew everybody else. I don't think it was a centre of high level crime, as if anybody dropped a bit of litter on the floor, the whole village would know who did it in an instant. It was quicker than social media is today, 50 years ago those Valleys were a hotbed of gossip, but even then you sensed this community spirit. If someone died, the whole village would rally around, and make sure that the family were OK. It was a trait I was to see throughout my time in the Valleys.

It was the first time it came across to me that I may be seen as different to others, groups of friends together was a trait of all schools even then, and did they want me in their gang because it was me or because I was the Policeman's son? Or was I to be rejected for the same reason, how many times was it said to me ' don't tell your dad' I can't recall, but it was endless, and this became a thread of my life which you will see throughout my story until I went to Cardiff in 1970.

After eventually leaving Glyncorrwg, for the only time in our lives, we actually lived in Maesteg, close to another of my aunts and uncles, Betty and Bill, and my cousin Janet.

My cousin Janet and I were the same age and close, we only lived just around the corner and Ivy a short walk away, and the family bond was as close as it ever was. I recall waking up one morning and there was snow everywhere. You can imagine the excitement but what followed was the long hard winter of 1962/3, which with houses of that time, were hard to keep warm, windows iced on the inside. Even I was getting fed up of this endless cold , schools were old buildings which meant you were freezing all day and it seemed to go on for ever.

4

Sundays were the worst day of the week to me and have been ever since for 2 reasons: firstly I was made to go to Sunday school, and secondly I had to go to my great aunt Gerties for Sunday dinner which I will explain later. Now I am not a religious person and never had been, I accept that some people are, my dad wasn't either but his sister and family were very religious. Anyway I went to the chapel, where my parents were married, Bethel, my Mum was always saying to me it was a Baptist church not Church of Wales, I never , and still don't understand the difference. All I remember is a dark, sparse, basic building with hard seats and someone shouting at me that I was going to be a sinner and God would save me. My uncomplicated enquiring mind did not help me see the logic of this as the chap who took bible classes found out, as I was the bane of that group by asking Why? and How?, and saying 'God will save you' was not washing it with me.

Like all Sundays at that time nothing, but nothing, was open. No pubs to drown your sorrows, or shops and even back then I would just wait for Monday to come around. The family unit was all that mattered, I have no recollection at that time of friends coming around, always family where the women bickered, argued, laughed, gossiped every weekend, all cousins in tow as well. There were 2 brothers Alex and Elwyn, Alex unfortunately died very young and sadly I have little recollection of him, but Elwyn was a character, like the Maesteg equivalent of Leslie Phillips, a bit of a charmer, and great fuel for the women's gossip time . He moved away and spent a lot of his life in Cardiff.

We spent a short time in Maesteg, just over a year and off we were again, to a place called Pontycymmer. It was a mining village dominated by the pit which was right opposite our Police Station up one of the steepest roads I ever remember. I was around 12 at this time, the regular trips to Maesteg continued regardless. Coming home at around Christmas time all I recall is sitting in the back of the car with my mum saying we had to count the number of Christmas trees we could see either side of the road. I always won. I have little recollection of this place apart for the fact that I started in Garw Grammar School here.

Off we went again at the end of 1965 to a place called Aberkenfig, which was close to Bridgend, the nearest we got to my Dad's home. I recall trips to Bridgend Rugby Club, where my dad had played and was still a well-known character there, and we never paid to get in. Dad went in for a few beers and left me outside. The highlight of the season was the local derby of Maesteg v Bridgend which would attract big crowds. I had split loyalties here, but in the end followed my Dad and was a Bridgend man for the rest of my life until the damn regions came in spoiling to some extent the community spirit of the town rugby club. Standing close to the ground watching the great players of the day was a real treat. At least it was flat there and the Maesteg link stayed as strong as ever. By the middle of 1967 we were off again to a Valley village called Ogmore Vale, which to me had no redeeming features apart from it was close to Nantymoel where long jumper Lynn Davies was from, I recall the welcome he had when he won the gold medal at the Olympics, open topped car with his medal on, an unknown world for most of those communities.

It was in Ogmore Vale I had my first taste of a job, there was a big and thriving bakery in the village which served the whole community in bread and cakes. It was amazingly called the Ogmore Vale Bakery. My Dad got me this job to earn a few bob, I must have been around 16 at the time. The first job they gave me was to put the cherries in the middle of cakes, yes this was what my education was for. These cakes came out of the oven and went along a conveyor belt and by hand I had to put these cherries, in the middle of these bloody cakes, from a big bucket of cherries next to me. Now they had to be in the middle, not just slightly off, but in the middle, and there was a bloke I suppose he was Head of Cherries ,on my shoulder all the time. Apparently it was a trial period in the Cherry Department, suffice to say it didn't last long. My boredom threshold was not very high in those days, and when the bloke went for a break I found myself standing about 3 feet back and trying to throw them on the cakes from a distance. I missed more than I hit. Head of Cherries would have thrown me out then, but as my dad was the local bobby he had to bite his tongue and suggested I tried something else. So my next job was egg washing sausage rolls, yes egg washing sausage rolls, again there was a conveyor belt and just before they went in the oven, I had to brush them with egg wash to give them a nice sheen when they were cooked. I was now with Head of Egg Washing, who was as impressed with me as the Head of Cherries was. When I started to draw faces and hearts etc on these sausage rolls, it was enough for him, another deep breath from him. In total less than an hour had gone now. The final straw with them was when I was sent to custard tarts, dear reader are you coping with the excitement here?

These were coming out of the oven in big blocks, and I had to cut them into well, custard tart sized pieces, they did have some sort of mark on them which showed me where to cut, but that was boring, so I was cutting big boys tarts which was about 3 times the normal size. Suffice to say a top-level meeting with the Heads of Cherries, Egg Washing and Custard Tarts, meant that despite the influence of dad, they suggested that this wasn't for me, I agreed and was out of the door and my total first employment had lasted just about half a day. Neither was a growing lad who thought he was Joe Cool going to wear a bloody hair net…. My dad in fairness shrugged his shoulders and that was the end of my temporary employment until Pontardawe.

To be honest we were there just over a year and I was beginning to get weary of this constant moving, you made friends, then moved on to make new ones. Then in the July of 1968 we moved to Sandfields estate where I am now a testosterone filled boy with plans in mind, this story in Sandfields will follow….

You will see from my early life why certain issues affected me, one my dad was a bobby, while most others were miners or steelworkers etc, I made friends and wondered did they want to be my friend because they liked me or because my Dad was an important member of the Community. For example, the issue often came to a head when girls came on the scene. I met one called Anne, nice enough and we got on well, but one day I overheard her mum saying to a friend she was pleased that ' her Anne' was going out with the ' policemans son' not a ' nice lad called Howard', it affected me more than I thought and my early life was lived with this uncertainty of whether they liked me as me or because of my dad . It was only when I went to Uni in Cardiff that that disappeared. Moving so often as I outlined above didn't make it easier either as I made some friends, and then forgot them as soon as I moved, not looking back had an effect. I didn't, and still don't to some extent, do nostalgia, school reunions passed me by, I have no recollection, and this constant moving didn't give me any roots. I cannot recall the names of anyone I went to school with until the 6th Form.

Oh, by the way I am 69 at the time of writing. I am just finishing many years of teaching and suddenly I felt I wanted to put these thoughts to paper, for me mainly, but maybe for others of that generation where it will trigger their own thoughts.

Summing this section up. My memories of the Valleys were not some image from 'How Green Was My Valley' with a bunch of blokes strolling up the main road singing Myfanwy in perfect harmony. My dad was the local bobby, and he was a person of some note in the community. When I was young around Christmas, you would open the front door and there would be a turkey, ham, bottles of gin etc on the doorstep. Police corruption now, but then given as a genuine gift, based on a virtue that you earn, respect, he was hard and fair and you can ask no more.

I suppose I must have been 10 before I found out that most people bought this stuff in shops, I just thought this would go on for ever, a bit of a shock when this stopped and we had to go to a shop to buy food. The other thing we had in the early days was a cell in the house, which was like an overnight cell, to move inmates on from the following day. In reality it was mainly full of local drunks as a place to sleep off before they were kicked out the following morning. My dad's warning that If I didn't behave I would be locked in there, it kept me on the straight and narrow. When you hear some of my later escapades, he would have put me in there and thrown away the key!!

My mum got paid to provide these guys with something to eat. Typical of my mum, she would give them what we would eat, many of the regular drunks who would be in on a Saturday night, would often say they looked forward to being nicked as it was the best apple crumble in the Valley!!

Living in a police station had its ups and downs, for example many Christmas days dad was on duty, although we were still at home. When he was Senior, on Christmas Day there would be a couple of police on duty and he would invite them in for a Christmas drink, most of them, especially the younger PC's would be happy with a small beer and were a bit nervous about coming into our private quarters, Dad being the kind of man he was would try and put them at ease. Then there was Sergeant Cooper. He had been in the force some time and was a tough uncompromising character, when Dad invited him in, he would often have ' a small whisky', now dad didn't drink shorts at all, so a small whisky was a large glassful... In about an hour or so, Sgt Cooper would do the whole bottle, but you wouldn't have known for one minute. He would then get up and go back to the station as if he had had a glass of shandy. We had all this whisky, vodka etc as gifts etc and they were stuck in a cupboard for years, as mum who was not a great drinker anyway, didn't drink it, and my dad was a beer man mainly. It would probably be the next Christmas waiting for Sgt Cooper to demolish it again. At the end of his shift, he would drive home and probably start again...You didn't argue with Sergeant Cooper, but he loved working for dad and had some great stories to tell, which I would laugh at, but not have a bloody clue what he was talking about. Just as well....

It was a novelty to eventually live in a house with no cell and buying our own Christmas stuff. I was always into music from a young age, like all of that time, Beatles, Stones, etc seemed the only bands around, I somehow , and can't remember how, started listening to American blues music and my life changed. I used to listen under my pillow at night, with a tiny transistor radio, the crackling sounds of Lightning Slim, Sonny Terry and Brownie Mc Gee and others and a new world opened up for me , as far from the Valleys as you could get... Remembering those early days in Wales is lost in the mists of time and you wonder what actually did happen compared to what you think happened but some memories are as vivid to me as if it was yesterday. From about 1964 on under my sheets with Radio Caroline was also a vivid memory, listening to Tony Blackburn, Johnnie Walker, Dave Lee Travis and they again opened my eyes.

My memories, as I mentioned, started to form in Maesteg. My grandad who used to work in the old paper mills in the area, lived with one of my aunts, about 5 doors down lived a great aunt and uncle, she was Gertie and lived with her sister Bessie. The house to be honest was scary, dark, basic and I used to hate going there. We used to have to go up on a Sunday for dinner, after Sunday School, where even at my young age the food was horrible, from that time on I never ever eaten gravy with a meal. All I remember was a brown sludge crawling over my plate. Gertie was also a big woman to put it politely.

Now at a young age you are told things which then confuse and baffle you. Gertie is a classic example, she was huge with a massive wart thing on her nose and really scary looking as well. Dad had drilled into me to always be honest and tell the truth, so we were around there one day after dinner, and I innocently turned to Gertie and thanked her for dinner and then proceeded to ask her why she was so fat and ugly. I recall a clip across the ear from my dad and told to apologise. Childhood confusion set in, I just said to Dad you told me to tell the truth and I get told off for it, apparently Gertie was fairly deaf, just as well, and then I went through life and realised we all live with these filters, ' that was a beautiful meal' (It was crap), 'you are looking well' (you have got fat) 'what a lovely dress' (Its cheap looking and hideous). I had to play these games when I was in situations where it was appropriate and as I have got older these filters have fallen off, and now I have reached my nadir, a grumpy opinionated rude old bastard, job done.....anyway to continue..

We would be over Ivy's who had my grandad, and the family congregated there on a Saturday. The men would be in one room watching the early days of Grandstand with Peter Dimmock, on a little TV, which consisted of wrestling, racing and rugby league ('up 'n under with Eddie Waring), they would organize a little bet and when the pubs were open, go and put a bet on and have a few beers as well.

My grandad had lost both his legs and was obviously bedbound. He lived for many years on a diet of whisky and Woodbines, under his bed were just fags and said whisky. He lived a remarkable number of years and eventually he got taken to hospital, where at about 80 he decided the fags were doing him no good, so he was going to give them up!!

He eventually died and the story was that the whisky had kept him alive by thinning his blood so much and that if there had been a breathaliser he would have failed it 2 weeks after he had died. Under his bed were endless bottles of whisky and woody's, I'm not sure what happened to them..... I had the socks which were at least unused...

Back to Maesteg... I was at an age where I was allowed to go into town on my own, 1 place I detested, the other was like the Tardis to me. First was the barber, in those days, not hairdressers, all I remember is an old man, usually with a filthy sort of mauve coat, with a fag hanging out of the corner of his mouth. I was thrilled with all these pics of hair styles you could theoretically have . The reality was that every cut was the same, short back and sides, sometimes straight if he didn't have a coughing fit during it…Then he would slap some Vitalis on it and it just looked like a greasy mess. I got cocky and one day and asked for a haircut like Adam Faith who was on one of these pics, it was cool with a greased quiff and looked the business. He just grunted started another fag and did the same short back and sides he had probably done for 40 years…

The other place was the record shop which had the booths where you could listen to records, it was heaven. I went in as often as I could on a Saturday, would ask to listen to whatever was popular at the time. In there I was transported to a world which I wanted to be part of, lights, glamour, glitz, fame, women crawling all over you, autographs , limos and endless money, then you went out back to the cold reality of a cold Valley town, devoid of any character to me in those days. The main industry was the local paper mills, where as I said my grandad used to work, hard tough uncompromising work. We lived in other small Valley towns where the mines were the main employer. I thought even then that was not something I would ever do, going down a hole just about big enough to crawl in, with all sorts of gasses, and just about every miner I came into contact with coughed from a combination of woodbines and coal dust, and life ended early for so many with Pneumoconiosis and lung cancer. Years later, I spent a significant part of my early life in Cardiff, watching how this bloody coal had been exploited by coal and ironmasters like the Crawshays of Cyfartha and the Butes in Cardiff. It made them rich but caused heartache in the Valleys where this coal was literally hewn by hand by hard people who became shells of men, often by the time they were 40 or so they were dead.

I cannot talk about my growing up period in the Valleys without talking about the 21st of October 1966, I was 14 at the time, living in Aberkenfig, and that day had a profound effect on me for the rest of my life. The Aberfan disaster.

Heavy Industry is by definition a dangerous field, and the people at the sharp end suffer untold dangers from the almost non-existent safety measures of the 19th century, mistakes and incompetence in the 20th plus the geology of the Welsh coalfields meant that Wales saw its share of horrors over the years.

Between 1851 and 1920 there were 48 disasters in the South Wales coalfield and over 3,000 deaths. In 1913 439 men died in Seghenydd, and even as late as 1960, 45 men died at Abertillery and in 1965, 35 men died at the Cambrian Colliery at Clydach Vale.

In these cases the communities pulled together to support and comfort,

But Aberfan was not men down a pit, it was 116 children and 28 adults who had just gone for a full day of lessons at school. Obviously in those days you did not have 24 hour wall to wall media coverage, dad knew first as the police were told that a 'major Incident' had happened, rumour and speculation was rife ,but when the full enormity of what had happened came out, you did not just have a small local community mourning, the whole of Wales was in a state of shock. I heard, and cried myself, thinking, it could have been me..I found out later through my dad, that many of the police and emergency services suffered long term mental health traumas after what they had seen. Now it would have a name, then it didn't. policeman dad knew were there, often had to leave, became alcoholics or sometimes even worse.

All of us who lived in that area were affected for life, every 21st of October, I stop and reflect, and a principle I live by which is live for today as tomorrow may not come, came from my experiences of that time.

Some of my next recollections of those early years revolved around the radio and TV of the time as the next chapter explains…

CHAPTER 2

MEMORIES OF TV AND
RADIO IN THE 60'S

The world changed in the 1960's with the introduction of the little box in the corner. The significant effect it was having on cinemas which were starting to decline, and Cardiff like everywhere else was seeing this effect , where the plethora of local cinemas was starting to turn into bingo halls.

I have to say that apart from the 60's I have never been an avid TV watcher as in the 70's as you will become aware, I was distracted by other things. Even now I rarely watch TV, I watch my sport on laptop . Mrs W is keeper of the remote anyway and she enjoys TV which is fine.

Anyway back to the 60's, even at the beginning of the 60's nearly three quarters of the population had a TV and by the end of the decade nearly the whole of the country had one, and the very rich more than one!!

It changed the whole layout of rooms as chairs and now sofas were now pointed to wherever the TV was, no remotes in those days, you had to actually get up to change channels, but given the fact there were only 2 channels it wasn't a complete hardship. A third Channel BBC2 arrived in 1964 but it was initially not very popular as it was seen to be a bit highbrow and posh.

Initially for me however my influences were from the radio, and what you listened to I believe moulded the type of humour you went on to appreciate. For me it was 'The Goons' something my parents didn't get, but used to make me cry with laughter. The chaotic, unscripted outgoings of Milligan, Secombe, Sellers and Bentine were to me a complete joy, at times I had no idea what they were talking about but I think neither did they!! Milligan was the catalyst of all this and his influences spread to Monty Python, plus John Lennon's irreverent humor was based on Milligan. The first record I bought was 'The Ying Tong Song' followed by ' I'm Walking backwards for Christmas'. Later I bought the books and records. What summed up Milligan was he insisted that on his gravestone was put: 'I told you I was ill'. He was buried in Ireland and the authorities insisted that the gravestone was in Irish!! It's why I went on to love the irreverent comedian Dave Allen plus as I said the Pythons in general and Cleese in particular with Fawlty Towers. It is amazing to think that there were only ever 12 episodes made, each one a classic.

I had to check some dates next but the recollections are mine , My earliest recall was 'Watch with Mother', although older people will remember 'Listen with Mother' on the radio. The wise and wonderful at the Head of the BBC decided that it could not be seen to be encouraging mothers to forgoe their domestic duties, so it was Watch WITH Mother, something you did together. Not Watch TV on your own, so mum could have the odd schooner of sweet sherry down her, so she could cope with screaming kids and shitty nappies. (I suppose it would be chilled Chardonnay now, but this was the 60's.)

As I recall, Watch with Mother had a cycle of different programmes on different days, most TV did not start until about 5.pm but watch with Mother had 2 short slots, about 11.00am and 1. Can't recall the actual days of each but Andy Pandy, The Flowerpot Men, Rag Tag and Bobtail and the Wooden Tops were the most popular, throw in Muffin the Mule and life could not get any better.

For me the world changed in 1965, I was 13 then, with the introduction of the Magic Roundabout. It was as brilliant then as it still is now. As background for this chapter I watched some old episodes of it and the depth and humor is still there, adapted from a French equivalent by Eric Thompson (father of Emma) the wonderful characters of Zebedee, Florence, Dougal the dog, Brian the Snail, Ermintrude the cow. Mr

McHenry the gardener and my favourite character of all time, Dylan the Rabbit. It immediately became a children's classic, and was brilliant on so many levels.

The Debate about whether Dylan was on drugs raged for years. I read a great story about what happened to Dylan later on. Apparently he made a fortune from the early days of Magic Roundabout, had all the trappings of success but spent his fortune on sex, drugs and rock and roll, the rest he wasted. He married Jessica Rabbit, she could cope with his womanizing but the drugs she couldn't cope with, so she divorced him and he then had no contact with his 326 children. Rumour has it that the rest of the cast had a whip round to get him some money for rehab but he blew that on drugs... I really want to believe that story, there were also stories around that he had infiltrated other characters with the odd spliff.

How do you explain otherwise 2 guys leaping out of a flowerpot shouting 'weeee' and talking to a weed? Also those who remember ' Tales of the Riverbank' with Johnnie Morris, I also loved ' Animal Magic' also with said Johnnie, and the talking mice etc, talking mice? Really? Dylan was behind that. Muffin the Mule, what is Muffin for God's sake, but let's move on here.

Mainly TV did not start until 5.00pm, apart from Saturday when Grandstand with Peter Dimmock was born, there was no afternoon TV. I've talked about Grandstand already. What else was popular in those days, my parents loved Dr Finlay's Casebook, The Black and White Minstrel Show (wonder why they don't show repeats of that these days?) Z cars and someone who I had forgotten who was popular in those days Millicent Martin, who was a very talented entertainer. Worked in Broadway and made her name singing satirical songs on a programme, which I was just beginning to get in to 'That Was The Week That Was' and went on to have 3 series of her own during that time. She is well in her 80's now and living in the USA. However the jewel of the crown in those days, from 1960, Coronation Street, more about that later.

For me it was the beginning of Doctor Who with William Hartnell and I was hooked to that for some time, of course Top of the Pops, which was normally on a Thursday and you waited with bated breath to see who was number one. I recall the celebration in 1965 when Tom Jones became the first Welshman in the modern era to have a number 1 with 'It's Not Unusual' and a year later another number 1 with 'Green Green Grass of Home'. It's amazing that he is still knocking it out at over 80.

I went off TOTP when the bubblegum crap appeared in the 60's and horror on horror my mother used to like it , especially the 'nice bands' like the Dave Clark Five. Who recalls Juke Box Jury with David Jacobs? which was normally the first show on a Saturday at about 5.00pm. 'I'll give it 5' became its catch line, can't remember the panelists but it drew huge audiences of over 10 million. I suppose it was the forerunner of X factor etc.

The first game show I can recall was 'Take your Pick' with Michael Miles and the announcer Bob Danvers- Walker and the 60 second yes/no game, where you couldn't say those words when questions were asked. It used to make me fall about. Then did you want to bid for 'Box 13' ? with the star prize or a booby prize, the tension was unbearable….

Then ' It's Friday, It's 5 to 5 ..It's Crackerjack!!' With Leslie Crowther and Peter Glaze. The initial presenter was Eamonn Andrews, but I recall it with Leslie Crowther from around 1964. It was hosted by many other famous(at the time) celebrities later, Michael Aspel, Max Bygraves, and Ed Stewart to name but a few. Oh how I wanted to go on to get a Crackerjack pencil (eventually changed to a pen) for every contestant who took part. I lost out in life as I had no Blue Peter badge OR Crackerjack pencil. How I got through my early life unscathed I'll never know….

Opportunity Knocks with Hughie Green was really a forerunner of 'Britain's Got Talent'. There was the introduction of the 'clapometer' to judge audience reaction, also the pubic voted for the winner by postcard!! Which had to be in your own handwriting (how they checked God knows). People who won included Freddie Starr, Paul Daniels, Les Dawson (who later hosted the show) Pam Ayres, Bobby Crush, Berni Flint and Little and Large.

Too many shows to mention which we didn't watch, The Saint being very popular, The Andy Williams show and American imports which were creeping in , Perry Mason, Bewitched to name but a few. I did get into Bonanza for a while but didn't stay with it, and they allowed American culture to creep into the UK.

I cannot write a piece about 60's TV without mentioning Coronation Street. On the face of it a series about a gritty back street in a poor Northern town would seem not to have a national appeal, but the country was hooked. The Rovers Return, Weatherfield, Newton and Ridley's Beer, became part of our lives. It was initially not a critical success when it started in December of 1960. By 1961 it was established as the premier TV series in the country and peoples schedules were changed to not miss the twice weekly show, of course no chance of recording then.

Why was it so popular? My view is that many of the original cast were brilliant character actors and actresses. You lived and breathed the characters. Pat Pheonix who played the brassy Elsie Tanner, and became the country's first TV sex siren, is a classic example . The other originals , Violet Carson's Ena Sharples was another , a trained actress of some note and the character was believable and almost a caricature of the old battle axe, with her faithfully underlings Martha Longhurst and Minnie Caldwell, who would put the world to rights in the snug of the Rovers. The Snobbish Doris Speed who played Annie Walker, and acted as if it was below her (later do you remember Hyacinth Bucket played by the wonderful Patricia Routledge, who reminded me of the Annie Walker character) and henpecked husband Jack Walker who just did what he was told, was a brilliant foil and wonderfully acted. Even Uncle Albert Tatlock played by Jack Howarth, created a character you could relate to.

The fact that I am writing this from my head with no notes is a testament to the brilliance of those people who I remember from nearly 60 years ago. Then there were the Barlow's Ken who remarkably is still there and the other Barlow's Frank, Ida and David. There were others, Leonard Swindley, played by Arthur Lowe, who went on to Dad's Army, Emily Bishop, previously Nugent ,played by Eileen Derbyshire for many years to name but a few. My parents would not miss an episode and they lived and breathed the goings on with everyone else. It was accused at one time of having no humour and later characters like the Ogden's, Stan and Hilda, plus Eddie Yates came along to introduce this humour. I recall a later episode when Stan died, it was a brilliant piece of acting by Jean Alexander on her own for 30 minutes, who deserved an award for an outstanding performance . Then the Mike, Ken , Deirdre saga which enthralled the nation for years.

I could go on but that is enough of Corrie for now , I'm sure all of you have your own recollections.

My final thoughts revolve around the Eurovision Song Contest. Until late 60's it had been won by various European Acts who I can't recall, but in 1967, the UK won for the first time with Puppet on a String and a barefooted Sandie Shaw, a quiz question now ,who were the other 4 UK winners of the contest? Put this book down and have a chat and think...............OK, times up. Answers Lulu 1969 with Boom Bang a Bang (tied), Brotherhood of Man with 'Save your Kisses for Me' in 1976 , Bucks Fizz with ' Making Your Mind Up' in 1981 and the one that many forget Katrina and the Waves in 1997 with ' Love Shine a Light'. How many of you will be cursing me for singing some of those all day....!!

I lost interest in it then until Terry Wogan started and gradually got more and more pissed as the programme dragged on, then making it worth watching. We can't even buy a point now....!

TV developed as the years passed. Morning TV for kids began with Noel Edmunds Multi Coloured Swap Shop with Keith Chegwin, John Craven and Maggie Philbin, and to me the more off the wall Tiswas, with Chris Tarrant, Sally James, Bob Carolgees and ' Spit the Dog' plus Lenny Henry and others, but that was to come later. This section for me is about The Goons, Watch with Mother .and the pinnacle for me ' The Magic Roundabout'. Hope this chapter triggers your own memories...

My constant moving around South Wales, which was a theme of my early life, continues...

CHAPTER 3

SANDFIELDS, PONTARDAWE, AND CARDIFF

We carried on moving until my Dad got posted on to the Sandfields estate in Port Talbot in 1968. I started A levels there at that time. We lived in the Police Station in the middle of a large council estate where around 20,000 people lived and nearly everyone worked in the Steel Works or Baglan Bay Petrochemical works.

I was slightly worried again. The school was slap in the middle of this estate and I worried about standards of teaching and discipline and went with some trepidation. My worries were totally unfounded, it was the best school I ever went to, standards of teaching were fantastic, and the care of staff was first class, uniform was strictly adhered to by everybody including the 6th form and the reputation of the school for sport was amazing.

The Rugby team were unbeaten for about 2 years, Wales forward, Alan Martin was a past player and a frequent visitor to the school. It was also unusual in the fact that it offered more than the traditional sports which tended to be rugby in the winter, cricket in the summer and athletics in between, but they also offered golf, volleyball and basketball. I tried them all.

The school were aware through my dad that I played both rugby and cricket, I was straight in the first team for both, but as ever it niggled away at me that it wasn't my abilities that got me in, but dad. I played the whole year, we were unbeaten and a 7's side I was part of won every tournament we entered. Training was intense , about 4 nights a week and it showed . About half that side went on to play first class rugby in Wales and 2 went on the books of Glamorgan cricket.

I had a great group of classmates in the 6th form, but I still suffered from this issue , do they like me because I was the policeman's son or my ability? But crucially by then that issue , for the first time in my life, had receded and I truly felt part of a group. It was with that team that I ventured on my first rugby trip .In my first year of A levels we went to Scotland to play a few games against local schools and watch the Scotland v Wales game at Murrayfield in the early part of 1969. Again a long bus trip but full of excitement plus the guys bonding was also important for me. We stayed with the families of the players, I cannot remember the guy I stayed with but I certainly remembered his drop dead gorgeous sister and his even more stunning Mum, let's call her 'Moira'. A Diana Dors lookalike whose husband worked away. I will not go into detail but just refer you to the story about Karen below....you will get my drift . I had a (not surprisingly) great weekend and my first Rugby trip to Scotland, was not to be my last as further chapters will explain. My philosophy was that education comes in many forms , experience them all. I never want to leave this world saying 'what if,' a philosophy I lived with was from a good friend who said 'never learn from your mistakes especially if you enjoyed them'. Mistakes I made many of them, regrets ? A few, but always a bit of a smile trying to slip through..

Oh by the way Wales won so all was well with my world at that time.

Now girls were well to the forefront and I fell in love daily. I met so many and a number I took back to the police flat we had, with girls that insecurity was still strong, I never really knew did they like me or was it because of my Dad. (You will have to read chapter 6 on Lily to find when this insecurity disappeared, but as that chapter will also show, other insecurities replaced them.)

Dear reader, one particular girl, her name was Karen took a shine and we were in the corner of the yard snogging as much as we were allowed. She was the first girl ever to invite me back to her house, the rest had been to mine, she lived on the Baglan estate nearby.

What happened next, happened to me more than once (read above), I went around dead nervous with some chocs in my hand for her mum. Knocked the door and her mum answered, she was drop dead georgous, (déjà vu?) she told me Karen was held up somewhere and come in and wait for her, my heart and a few other places, were beating now…Can't remember her name but she told me her husband was working away from home, my lips were dry by now and a hot flush was coming on…. Karen rang home to apologise and she was stuck in Swansea and she would see me in school the following day and rearrange.

Modesty stops me going into detail, but again my education was extended greatly, left about 2 hours later, tired and drained , and suddenly realised I had forgotten to give her the bloody chocolates… At this point dear reader , I must emphasise that this did not become a regular activity, just the 2 incidents happened to be close together. You wait for a bus for hours and then 2 come along at the same time. To my knowledge this never happened again ……except….

When I got home my mum asked me if I had a good night, before I could answer, I beetled into my room and stayed there till the morning, went to school and met Karen and said that it was time to move on, she had met someone else anyway, saw her in school but did I see her mum again? I'll let you dwell on that one…

That was a high but there was a crushing low. I was now regularly going to the Top Rank in Swansea and as you do I met a girl in there who lived in Aberavon, she was lovely and we had a great night, her dad was picking her up and I asked for a date the following week, she readily agreed, 14th time I had fallen in love that month but hey ho..

I was truly excited , bought a new shirt and shoes (mum did), tidied up , checked my after shave and clean pants and walked to where we had arranged to meet about 15 minutes early.

The set time passed and I wasn't too bothered initially. I waited and waited, of course no way to get in contact, I waited for a full hour and realised I had been stood up, I was gutted and had never had this rejection before and walked home to my parents with my tail between my legs . Mum saw I was upset and tried to console me but dad just said , 'there are plenty of fish in the sea so bugger her'. Mum then giving him one for swearing at me and my 11 year old sister asking what bugger meant...

Then came a difficult time, I was settled and happy in school for the first time ever, my work was coming on in leaps and bounds, and I was to be one of the Head Boys in the last year.

A few things I learnt when I was in Sandfields, mainly from my dad again. He had never smoked and I was getting to the age of peer pressure where some of my friends did smoke. I was old enough then for my parents to go out and leave me at home . They had a drinks cabinet and a few ciggies and cigars for visitors. You will remember when you wanted to drink a bit of your parents' Whisky, Gin Vodka etc, but wondered whether they had marked the level that was in the bottle and they would know .Great psychology then from dad, he threw a packet of fags at me and told me to help myself to drinks. I originally thought I was in heaven, smoked about a packet of fags, tried all the shorts and after a few hours you can imagine how I felt. I threw up for most of the night and felt like absolute shit for days afterwards. I would be a liar to say I didn't drink or smoke ever again. I had the odd cigar, but never smoked cigarettes and yes I drank, but never shorts, just beer and later wine. In fact I started smoking a pipe , a strange thing to do at 18 in those days, but perhaps I just wanted to be different even then. I smoked a pipe for many years and enjoyed it greatly, but never inhaled. Thank you again dad.

Went home to be told we were moving again, Dad had been promoted to Pontardawe in the Swansea Valley, and at that point I hated the bloody police force.

This was now a problem, I was half way through my A levels and did not want the disruption of another school. We were incredibly lucky to find a teacher who taught in Sandfields and lived close to Pontardawe and drove me in each day and my time in Sandfields continued.

Suffice to say I did well at my A levels, for a school on a council estate we had one of the best A level results in Wales, a number went to Oxbridge and the vast majority of us went to wherever we wanted. Never judge a school by its cover.

Some brief stories in Pontardawe, it was then a small, typical Welsh valley town, Police Station on the main road and the local pub, The Ivy Bush, a bit further up and if I was to know anyone I had to join the cricket club, as most of my friends were in Sandfields. I never played Rugby there, joined and enjoyed my cricket and a lot of the boys would go to the Ivy Bush for a beer or 2 after the game, I was still 17 and with my dad the local bobby, everybody knew him and me. To the eternal credit of my dad he had a quiet word with the landlord and said it was OK to serve me, as it was my Dad's watering hole on a Friday, no police ever checked anyway.

Did I take advantage of this opportunity? Damn right I did, the very first night I went up on my own, sat at the bar , and proceeded to get merrily pissed as a parrot with no problem at all.

It came time to go ,now home wasn't far, so I took a deep breath, bit left and right but I was vaguely going in the right direction. Problem was I was dying for a pee and had left my keys in the bar. I got to the front gate, needed a pee in the garden and decided to ring the bell at the same time , not my best idea..

The door was opened by my Mum, I peed on her shoes, fell over and had to get carried to bed..

Not the finest moment of my life and it was some time before I was allowed out again... anyway summer of 1970 had arrived and my A level results popped through the door. My mother could not look , no one had ever been to Uni before in our family, so it was a big deal to them. I had had this accident so I was in plaster and my plans to do sports in Loughborough was down the pan. My A levels were good, it was Economics in Cardiff, so dear reader my next stop in the September of 1970 was the bright lights of the big city and then the fun and frolics really began.....

A footnote here, I did well for the cricket side and I was often mentioned in local press articles, 5 wickets here, or 50 runs there. I did not realize that my Dad collected and kept these press cuttings. Many years later when I think he knew he was very ill, through the post came this envelope, with just a quick note saying I think you will want these, and there were all these cuttings which I put away, not too long after that he died. Those cuttings are still a treasured possession of mine, not because they remind me of my success as a cricketer but how my Dad kept them all those years....

Before I move on to the twinkling lights of Cardiff, some recollections of holidays in those days especially visits to Porthcawl and the yellow brick road to Pontins...

CHAPTER 4

PORTHCAWL AND HOLIDAY CAMPS

Writing this book always meant to me that I was seeing that period through my eyes and memories that I recall. It is likely very different for others, but this is my perception. The most abiding holiday and day trip memories for me were initially visits to Porthcawl. From the endless maelstrom of the biggest beach I had ever seen to Coney Beach amusements, Trecco Bay, the big dipper, endless fish and chip shops, bars, ice cream parlours, crazy golf and much more . One big factor was that my grandfather lived there and worked in a shop renting and selling caravans, he was a friend of Jimmy Theodore who was the king of caravans in those days. My great grandmother was still alive then and lived in the town, a fearsome frightening woman who used to scare the living daylights out of me, and I recall she used to pull the sofa out and I had to stay behind there as it was my 'play area' I was bloody terrified and I would be stuck there for hours, scared even to ask for a pee, my sister told me that my mam was not happy with this either.

Back to my grandfather, he ran a caravan shop, which as I mentioned, sold and rented caravans which were incredibly popular then. He used to let me and my sister sit in these caravans, they were wonders to behold to me , like palaces on wheels, but years later I must say they were not my most favourite places to holiday.

It may be worth a bit of background here. There was a time in the 1830's that the coal trail came to Porthcawl, albeit on a very small scale. Porthcawl point became the terminus of a horse drawn carriage bringing iron and coal from the nearby Llynfi valleys around Maesteg. It was a fraction of the iron and coal that came down from Merythr to Cardiff,

Swansea and Newport ,but was enough for a docks in Porthcawl to be built in the mid 19th century, but the weather on that part of the coast was difficult and the docks closed in the early 20th century. Then as Industry declined , tourism was starting to grow. The first seeds were after WW1 where the population of the town increased plus more in the summer season, then infrastructure started to grow with the grand pavilion appearing first, Then in the 1920's Coney Beach was built, initially for US troops after WW1. It was called Coney Beach as there was a similar entertainment centre in New York with the same name. Many years later I took Lily once(more about Lily later), and she laughingly reminded me that this was a bit different to the one in New York!!. The main beach was such that it was a nightmare to go swimming, as the tides meant that the sea was such a long way away, you could not even see anybody by the seafront when you were sitting on the beach, plus there were dangerous currents, but it was flanked by Trecco bay and the more sedate and genteel Rest Bay. With Trecco Bay came the endless rows of caravans which were packed in what was miners fortnight, last week of July and the first week of August.

Many from Cardiff will remember packed stations with endless streams of people pouring down from the valleys. The station full of battered suitcases that often only came out once a year and kids clutching an often handed down bucket and spade .I recall being there at those times with packed pubs of men who spent 50 weeks of the year in hard dangerous graft, having 2 weeks of release from it, where fresh sea air was a novelty and the pubs were overflowing and they bloody deserved every minute of it. Whole streets would have caravans in the same row, just replacing the small Valleys houses they lived in. If you were up to no good, go the Valleys in Miners fortnight, a ghost town, no shop was worth opening, police weren't busy and there was an eerie silence. This was the backdrop of a place as a kid I loved..

As was the case with many Valley families in the 60's we went on holidays and trips as a big family group. Aunts, uncles, cousins and a few great aunts if they could make it, as long as they got the best deck chair. Loved those deck chairs, took hours to put up. Always packs of sandwiches, crisps and , a little limp by then, sausage rolls ,and warm fizzy pop!! Going in Coney Beach was like Alice through the looking glass, first thing that happened was you got completely soaked from the water slide which was just by the entrance. The smell was intoxicating, endless fish and chip shops, candy floss in that sickening pink colour, just flavoured sugar, but just melted in your mouth, toffee apples ,all swallowed with a warm bottle of Dandelion and Burdock pop, Corona's finest. Got extra from the pop lorry when it came around and you knew that a day trip was close. Life could not get any better, perfect, and still enough room for a bag of chips with some unidentified fish, just well...fish.

Me and my cousins would be round there wanting to go on everything and try everything, knocking cans down with a ball, you had no chance as the bottom row of cans was glued to the shelf, but it didn't matter. There was a tombola and I remember winning some sort of teddy bear which would be banned now, eyes stuck in with pins, but again, watching the stilt man advertising the circus that would suddenly appear . Then desperate to get in the queues for the bumper cars, so you could smash into your cousin or uncle. My dad was incredibly competitive and would not let anybody else win. Being told off by the attendant for bumping too much, he once took out his police identity card as if his juristiction covered a bumper car in Coney Beach .Anyway back to my prize, in the end it was MY prize and I would hang on to it for grim death until I dropped it, or more likely was sick on it. End of the day winning some poor goldfish in a bag, poor bugger was normally dead by the time we got to the car, never ever got one home.

Heady days, simple delights, no electric arcades screwing you out of a lot of cash, it was honest fun, the aunt's mainly kept an eye on us, as Uncles were knocking it back in one of the endless pubs. No breathalisers in those days, but later in the day packed all the stuff, back in the charabanc and back home, asleep in about 5 minutes , until you woke up and wanted a pee or the chips, crisps, candy floss, toffee apples hot egg sandwiches and gassy pop were beginning to cause a rumble in the jungle.....

For Cardiffians I imagine it was similar going to Barry Island, but for us from the Valleys, the end of the yellow brick road was Porthcawl. Looking at my dad's picture in my room, thinking of him lying in the sand and us trying to bury him in it. He was a big man and all of us ,him included, loved it. He was the gentlest giant you could ever meet, caused me innocent laughter over what now seems silly times, but as you get older it is easy to get cynical, I don't, and have an unashamed tear in my eye every time I recall those days, and it was another piece in the never ending jigsaw.

Another holiday memory of the time in those days centred on holiday camps . Even as I got older we still went on holidays as a big group, but the earlier ones usually meant 3 or 4 cousins plus maybe 6 adults, we used to go to holiday camps in Devon. Mainly we used Pontin's as my mum thought it was 'posher' than Butlins, These holidays started for us with 3 or 4 cars , wending our way towards the Aust ferry, the Severn bridge would come a while later . For me it was always a delight, even the short ferry trip was a thrill and it felt like I was on a large cruise liner. Used to stand at the front and think I was the captain. The fact you could see our destination made no difference, to me it might have been crossing the Atlantic. Sometimes on bad weather days the ferry would rock and roll a bit, and I don't think health and safety was paramount. Once we were the other side as my mother would say we were now ' down England way' the excitement really started although there was still a distance to go, the same as Porthcawl trips, there were endless packets of (hot) sandwiches, with spam, potted salmon spread (which was posh), and some form of cream cheese, and someone had made a pudding or treat of treats like Arctic roll, which by now was an Arctic mess.... An aside, I made the mistake when I was very young of telling my grandmother I liked the skin on rice pudding (I didn't) so for ever afterwards it was always my treat to have this globule of dark skin put in my dish first, even my mother thought I liked it so she gave it to me as well!! I think there was a smirk from my sister who had the proper stuff underneath. Have to say have not eaten rice pudding since, My grandmother also knew that I also liked bread and butter pudding, by that I meant slices of bread with raisins in milk and cooked till crispy, I did (and still like that) and my mum cooked it well also, but my grandmother had another version which was just bread pudding, this was a different kettle of fish altogether, how it was made, God only knows, but it was like a house brick and about as hard to cut and eat. I'm sure Wimpy's bought a pile of them to make the walls in their new houses in Bridgend. Going to my grandmothers was a toss the coin moment, bread or bread and butter pudding...

You know this book is rock and roll when you have spent almost a whole page talking about bread and butter pudding. Sex , drugs and rock and roll it isn't

Anyway the excitement would rise as the usually wooden sign saying 'Welcome to Pontin's', appeared, in through the gate to what looked like a scene from a war movie, remember when I was small watching 'Escape from Colditz' with John Mills, and wondering would we need to build a tunnel to get out? We would get our key to Stalag 2 or whatever, drop off the cases and stuff and then off for a tour of the camp. Dad logging where the bars were and going to the opening meeting in the main stalag ballroom to be told the rules that had to be followed or you would incur the wrath of the camp commandant. Times of breakfast would be announced on the tannoy and each days fun packed itinerary would be announced which you felt obliged to go to with your friendly blue coat who had a stuck on smile, probably because he was pissed from the night before after dealing with endless moaning parents and sniveling kids who had lost their teddy or whatever. In hindsight the T V series Hi Di Hi was bang on the nail. Me? I loved it, I would want to do every competition, every swimming gala, darts, snooker competition I could. It was always a split holiday, our parents wanted rid of us, and we did not want these uncool older people spoiling our fun either.

My Dad was often the ringleader, leading the rest on their jolly japes around the camp (is it hereditary and did he pass on to me?) Many of you who may have been to these camps will have your own recollections, mine were the calls at 8.00am on a tannoy to go to breakfast if you were in chalets 1 to 100 or whatever, and in a dining hall which had the charm and appeal of Wormwood scrubs, then the list of games for the day, with some bluecoat encouraging you to knobbly knees or whatever (he or she had the short straw) I loved it…We were encouraged to take part by our parents , mainly as they were heading for the bars as soon as they opened, dad normally in front, with beer, the early days were bottles of mild or bitter, but the days of keg beers were soon with us, Watneys were dominant with the infamous Red Barrel, then things like Double Diamond appeared, lager was around in the 60's but not so much, Carling Black Label, Worthington E and Harp lager had started, but the lager boom really started in the 70's after the package holidays to places like Benidorm took off.

To my dad it didn't matter, he would normally be the first up singing and I would eventually join him on some of the later trips . He had a extremely rude version of ' Green grow the rushes o' which I joined in with relish, with my mum with her head in her hands, but a few Port and Lemons or Babyshams and she didn't care either. They all drank and smoked as most did in those days, but for some reasons most of my uncles or my dad never smoked, and that is probably why I never have either. The night usually finished with my Dad leading a Conga through the bar to wherever he fancied. We had to share a cabin , a bit like Colditz and my recollection is my dad snoring like God knows what until that bloody tannoy started at 8.00 the following morning…

It was uncomplicated basic accommodation, the entertainment was often of a low standard but did people enjoy it? Yes they did. Watching my mum and dad gliding around the dance floor was a joy to see, for a biggish man he moved really well and the enjoyment on their faces was palpable and clear. It was an age of innocent fun, never saw any trouble despite the vast amount of beer that was consumed and for many it was that few weeks away from the reality of cooking , cleaning, shopping , kids and worry. Yes life has moved on but those holiday camps were a valuable part of 50's and 60's life and Billy Butlin and Fred Pontin got it just about right. Stick a youngster in there now and all they would be looking for is the wifi code and spend their day indoors playing video games. If I sound like an old fashioned fossil then I plead guilty, but the importance of them to me growing up is that I still recall the unbridled fun and enjoyment I had when I was young. I make no apologies at all.

Later on in the 60's, we still went to various Devon Camps, but the accommodation was better by that stage and the big family groups had gone different ways now and we had gone with other friends. By 1966 the Severn Bridge had opened and getting there was a lot easier. You are at that crucial age where you feel you should be doing stuff on your own but still no money to do that so you relied on your parents. I think my parents had realised that those days were naturally coming to an end anyway. I believe the last one we went on was a place called Barton Hall. It used to be privately owned but was sold to Fred Pontin and it became Pontin's flagship centre to compete with Butlins. Fred Pontin was an astute business man and saw the growth of foreign holidays and opened the Pontinental group also.

I must have been about 15/16 and hormones were beginning to appear, and I was allowed there to go with a guy I met for a drink on my own, it was my first beer (with my parents knowledge) and we felt like cocks of the North, up to the bar 2 pints of Watney's Red Barrel..and there were a couple of girls there about our age giggling over a Babysham, glancing at us, now I was in a quandary…I was given enough money for a couple of beers, but I had a bit of my own, do I sidle over offer to buy them a drink click my fingers, wink and off we went to the back of the equivalent of Barton Hall's bike sheds,….nah. Took me about an hour to sidle across somewhere near her and came out with that knicker dropping line , 'where are you from' and in the end she said something like Canterbury, I said 'that's nice', then stunned silence, off she went with her white plastic boots and cheap skirt, never to be seen again.

Everything you do at that age you learn from, suffice to say if you read the chapter when I was in Sandfields, it never happened again, anyway I had enough for 4 beers drank them all, had a pee in the shrubs and beetled back to the chalet. At least we weren't sharing. I think I might have been with sis, so tucked my hormones away for another day….

That was the end of an era, last holiday together but over the years I had had a great time with them, But when one period finishes another starts, and boy it did…..

Next we move on to the twinkling lights of the big City, well it was big to me, Cardiff. And there dear reader many things took place and the people and places I met and saw there, were to change my life forever….

CHAPTER 5

HELLO CARDIFF, NICE
TOO MEET YOU..

So I arrived in University in the September of 1970, to supposedly study Economics at the newly built Tower block. This was obviously not my first visit to Cardiff. My first visit was in the bitterly cold winter of 1963, I was 11 and for Christmas my dad had bought us tickets to go and watch England v Wales at the Arms Park on the 19th January. It was a miracle the game took place at all, 30 tons of hay, braziers, shortening the pitch etc meant they played the game. It was one of the few live sports played at that time, no way would it have taken place these days. I was beside myself with excitement, each day I crossed off the day on my calendar, then after a sleep free Friday we were off. I recall driving along (an icy) A48 and Cardiff was getting closer and closer. Those of you of my generation will remember the 2 TV masts, as you got closer to Cardiff. I found that when the 2 masts were together and looked like one mast, then you were at the exact top of the hill before you drove down towards Culverhouse Cross, then you could see Cardiff on the horizon and I was beside myself. Through Ely, down Cowbridge Road and into town. Kick off was at 3 and I did wonder why we were there at about 10.00 am. Dad said it was to be able to park, if you were that early you could park in front of the castle which we duly did. Years later I realised Dad had a set routine, he would head towards the police club in Cardiff and I was told to wait outside ' for a minute'. This is a Welsh minute, I didn't mind, but there was some sort of reception which no doubt included a few beers, then it was up St Mary St, in and through the Market, just about at the time the doors of the Old Arcade opened, he seemed to know a lot of people

35

and this was part of his pre match ritual. I was told to sit outside for a short while, I was so excited I didn't care, I had never seen so many people, noise and colour ever ,and was transfixed. He popped out every so often gave me a few pence and let me go on my own, into the market to buy cockles from Ashtons, I felt so grown up!! Then I got back and the singing started and Dad was back out with some more money and told me to get some dinner (It was breakfast, dinner then tea NOT breakfast, lunch and dinner!!) Off I went and this time it was faggots and peas and a coke, I felt that life could not get much better than this.

Fair play to dad he popped out regularly to see if I was OK, eventually he and a few of his mates came out and I thought that we were off to the game, but he had booked a table in the Model Inn, upstairs and again I was outside , but I didn't care, the noise, the smell of beer (which I eventually got used to myself) people singing, buying burgers, sandwiches from a big pile from the endless street sellers around the ground, myriad rugby shirts and scarves, red and the occasional white, was a world that was all new to me and I loved it…

Many years later, towards the end of my Dads live visits I was living in Cardiff , so all train and bus, (breathaliser then) I took him and tried to follow the same sequence as he had done years ago but just him and I , a few beers in the Arcade and I booked a table in the Model Inn and we had a really special time, he was getting ,and starting, to look old, didn't drink too much and wanted a sleep, we had good seats then and it was Wales in the 70's and they won easily. I was so glad we did it, he owed me nothing but we never did it again and that will forever be there.

Going back to the original game in 63, we had no seats, in a cold, packed, (I think) East Terrace, I could see nothing , so he got me to the front against the fence, then put his arms either side of me so I wouldn't get crushed, I thought not much about it then, but later it put in stark reality what being a good dad is, protecting your children and the significance hit me a few years after his death and I unashamedly cried for days…

I am sitting writing this opposite a picture of my dad, he was a big Rotarian and Mason, and it is a picture of him holding a cup up on a visit to the Millenium stadium with one of those groups, It is a treasured possession and takes me back to that day he protected me in a cold Arms Park in 1963.

There were other visits , mainly into the Centre with my mum, whose whole wardrobe was basically from Marks and Spencer, I learnt so many tricks from my dad, he hated shopping so he would find some reason to ' go and buy a magazine' or 'look at records'. Mostly he knew the nearest watering holes, he loved the Taff Vale or the Park Vaults, but anywhere close would do, I used to remind him to buy a magazine or my mother would rumble his plan, she wasn't stupid and I'm sure she knew but normally we got away with it .

Head forward 7 years and I was now on my own for the first time in my life, parents were not around and I was suddenly sharing a house with 11 complete strangers, who were to become friends quickly, we were all in the same boat with plenty of distractions afoot, most of which I tried over the next few years plus some I invented myself . My initial problems were due to the fact that I had had a serious leg injury and turned up to College in plaster and crutches which was an impediment, but not as bad as it could have been and it did not last a long time. To that point in my life I had been a bit of a loner, moving houses and schools regularly with my dad as a bobby meant I had no particular roots. Friends were very transient, they came and went. Academically I was quite bright and took a shine to Economics for some reason, although I did want to go to one of the PE colleges especially Loughborough or Millfield as sport was my passion, but my leg injury, (I'll talk about that later) put paid to that, then I needed to go to a reasonably close university, didn't want to go to Swansea as it was too close to home, so Cardiff it was, so my time in Cardiff was just by chance and luck, but life is just a series of ' what if's', is it not?

So there I am in Glynrhondda St, mam had to make my bed and be sure it was clean and tidy as I had a ground floor room with another Welsh guy called Kelvin. Now Kelvin. I was initially limited in my activities by spending as I explained , much of my early time on crutches. I moved into 32 Glynrhondda Street, to mix with a fairly eclectic group of guys who I will talk about as we go on. I got into student accommodation, which was not normal for first year students, but because of my situation I got into this house. My first room mate as I said was Kelvin, to be honest I don't remember much about him, we shared a room because he was on crutches as well, we became affectionately known as 'Cripps Corner'' To this day I had no idea what he was doing in College but he had 2 major things going for him, somehow he had more money than the rest of us put together and secondly he had a television, deep joy. It was rented by his mother who I met only once, ' Its service you get when you rent your colour set from..........(bet those of an age are singing this now and it will niggle at you for days !)

None of us were particularly worried about the state of the house, there was a hoover, but I have no recollection of using it. But Kelvin was another case altogether, the first day of term he put his sheets etc on his bed, the next time they came off was the end of the first term, they came off on their own, stiff, also he ate all his food in bed. If you wanted to know what food was available you did not need a menu , just a quick look at Kelvins' sheets would have given you what he had eaten (and drunk) for the last few months.

Taking people back was a no no, my fantasy of endless nubile students rushing into my bedroom was spoiled by the fact that I could only operate on one leg and I shared a room with the beast from the swamp. Being amorous on one leg is a fine issue of balance and did not work to well in the early stages, you hoped you would meet a girl who had broken the opposite leg, so balance was possible, but no.

My First night there we had to find the Students Union, I now know how Dorothy felt going down the yellow brick road… I would get to know that walk in my sleep, down Senghenydd Rd, under the bridge , left into Dumfries Place, which was all houses then, and into the Union which was always going to be the first call in my ' Bermuda Triangle' which I will explain later. I was hooked .Students of all colour, creed and nationality mingling together, the Rhondda it wasn't !! It had taken me some time to get there on crutches so a seat was always available, I had never seen so many attractive women in one room at the same time and rich pickings were there, we were all in the same boat, mostly all away from home for the first time and I was good at milking my broken foot for all it was worth. A drunken night followed, but we decided to go for a walk, or limp in my case, into town, the old Alexandra Hotel was being gutted then, soon to be the Pig and Whistle, so off we went , Taff Vale was first, then crossed the road to the Park Vaults, then someone said there was a students club around the corner , hello Monty's, plus a 'posh ' place next door Qui Qui's, now I had just had my term's grant from the college, I quickly realised this grant was not going to last a term, in fact it would be lucky if it would see out the week. Monty's became a home from home, I became a bouncer there and many stories to tell.

After Monty's the next stop was El Greco's to normally sleep on a steak, sometimes on these first exploratory trips, I had forgotten my crutches and was walking on my plaster cast, which was the start of regular visits to the CRI to have my plaster fixed, the best thing they did was to put like a rubber thing at the bottom which I could walk on….

There would be movements out of this triangle, especially as I went down the docks, I loved music and I heard about this guy Vic Parker who played in the Quebec in the docks area, again my life would change down there.

The last thing I had said to my parents with a straight face that I would be a good boy, work hard and behave. I did not even get 1 out of 3...I decided quite early on that me and Cardiff were made for each other, we had things each could offer, and believe me I did. It started a relationship that went on for over 17 years and still is there which is why I am writing this.

In the first year like all students around where I lived, we used the Woodville, Mackintosh, Union, Claude etc which were predominantly students pubs, where a meal out was from a jar of pickled eggs, or if it was posh a scotch egg...or the cockle man would come in.

I really enjoyed that don't get me wrong, plus I knew my way around town pubs, Taff Vale, Park Vaults, Rummer, Bluebell, Griffin , Philarmonic etc , up to the Cambrian and Terminus, but on my 'alone' days towards the Docks and Bute I would head.... If it was the evening I would walk across the road from the Terminus and enter my Tardis, in the early days I had a game, I had a coin in my hand and when I walked down a road I would toss it and if it was heads I would go right at the next junction, tails left, sometimes on a whim , straight on.

I knew early on that it would not be long for me to hit a pub or club. Now this was not my world and I would be a liar if I said there was no flutter in my tummy when deciding to go in or not, my recollection was that there always seemed to be a pub on a corner, or in the middle of a terraced street. I cannot remember the names of all these, some stick, the Mount Stuart, Marchioness of Bute, the Red House to name just a few.

In many ways the pubs had similar set ups, a number of small separate rooms, public bar, lounge bar, 'the snug' , or as in the early days of the valleys there were also men only rooms . I always headed for the public bar, the lounge was often the same with a bit of mat on the floor... I might as well have the word 'student' written in neon on the top of my head it was that obvious. I remember things from the Valley days, that you could not just sit on a spare seat as that was 'Jim's' or 'Tom's' chair. I remember walking in to my first bar, busy, full of smoke, tables of small groups, they glanced at me thinking who is this, and looking behind me to see if it was a bunch of us on some sort of jolly, when they realised it was only me, they lost interest.

I would look for somewhere to sit, always take a book or paper so I didn't seem to be staring at people but I did want to just look. It was the days when the lifeblood of Cardiff was SA Brains, so SA, Bitter or Dark it was, you would not ask if the Chardonnay was chilled, not the days of wine down there, city centre pubs started those big wooden barrels, but the concept of chilled wine was not an option, warm red or white it was.

I would order normally a pint of bitter to start, say nothing, give my money and sit quietly, they were the days of dominos, cards, remember bar billiards? And a shelf with shove ha'penny board. Watching guys play dominoes, which I became fascinated in, cards, and often tables with guys of various creeds and colours, talking close together, and passing stuff to each other, what I did not know, they were furtively looking around to see who was there, I kept my head down, I felt no aggression to me at all, mild curiosity and indifference mainly, but the beer was normally good.

Those of a certain age will remember that in 1970 these were the days of pre decimalisation, where there were 240 pence (with a d not p) to the pound 20 shillings to the pound. Decimalisation took place on the 15 February 1971, we had been warned for a few years this would happen, but older people would find it difficult to go from pounds, shillings and pence and things divisible by 12, to pounds and pence divisible by 10. This memory came about because I read an article in February of 2021 of how it was 50 years since this new currency started, most beer in those days was less than 2 shillings a pint, so going out with a pound and a 10 bob note, would potentially give you 15 pints or more!! Deep joy. I remember beer in the union was about 1/10d a pint, no wonder we had such good nights.

Remember in the early days of Lily (she is to come), who would burst in say hi to everyone, ask the barman or woman who would they take dollars, and cause a ruck if they didn't have Southern Comfort... In the end though they all loved her, and as will become obvious, so did I....

I would do this maybe 3 days a week always had to be on my own in the early days, same routine, toss a coin to decide where to go, eventually the Quebec became a regular haunt, not only the nights when Vic Parker or The Icons were playing but ordinary nights, as time went by I did meet people who I still remember, being pulled in to play darts one night, and becoming a star of the local domino's league!!

I wasn't a Docks boy, but I felt comfortable there, nostalgia is not always 'the good old days' housing was starting to be knocked down for the Butetown redevelopment, jobs were scarce, and fairly menial and low paid, but me and that particular part of the City, nodded at each other and developed an understanding.

As I mentioned earlier I hit this problem. I was there to study Economics, work hard and behave , which were my mothers last words before she left , which were still ringing in my ears. This lasted about 2 hours before , I don't know whether it was a conscious or unconscious decision to say that for this first year, too much college was going to encroach on the time that I needed to have fun, so studying took the back seat, but for far longer than I anticipated.

My philosophy in life was if I did something to give it 100%, I gave enjoying the delights of Cardiff far more than 100%... as you dear reader, will find out. It was about 3 months before I went into the Uni library and that was only to meet a girl!! I was on the 8th floor of the tower block, it didn't take them long to wonder who the hell I was, and my personal tutor pretended he remembered me, but had no clue who I was... In my whole university career I never owned a text book, somehow I had some skill of Economics and would rather develop my own theories and ideas than some

50 year old theory by some old fart who was probably dead by the time I was supposed to look at his antiquated theories.

The problem was the few lectures I had were in the morning, I didn't do mornings , having normally just got home and ready to sleep all day before starting fun and frolics all over again.

To continue my Cardiff 'Bermuda Triangle', sometimes these trips included others but often just myself and see what happened on the way.

It was basically a pub crawl through town, down Queen Street, some pubs in the Kingsway then up St Mary Street to the Terminus, then it was decision time, back or towards the come hither twinkling lights of Butetown and the docks . I have regailed you of when I went on my Docks sojurn, it was a Bermuda Triangle because for me I never knew when I was going to come out. I had some calling points on the way home, which in my early days meant I may not reappear for 3 or 4 days or so, and I will give you an example of the early pub crawls and there you will meet Alun....

After Alun it would be good for you to meet some of my early friends, especially Walt , Teo and last, but certainly not least, Lily.

CHAPTER 6

ANATOMY OF A CARDIFF PUB CRAWL and ALUN

A pub crawl was almost a right of passage in 1970's Cardiff. It was easier then with the vast amount of drinking establishments that were on offer going down Queen St, Pig and Whistle/ Taff Vale/ Park Vaults and many others, across the other side of the Road at times, down the Kingsway for the Rose and Crown, across the Road to the Rummer Tavern, then start your way up St Mary St, with the Albert, Bluebell, Philharmonic, Cambrian to the Terminus and then down the yellow brick road towards the Docks. What was the logic of these events? Why not stay in one place, get comfortable and stay there? Tradition and logic at cross purposes. These events had to be carefully timed and organized. At this time which was still in the early days, my life had fallen in to some sort of pattern by then , I had a growing number of friends, male and female, who had the same attitude as me at that time, no work , all play and we could have a night/day out at a moment's notice. Maybe someone's birthday, or their budgie's birthday was good enough for a crawl. I did many of these most of which I can't recall, but an early one stands out in my mind now as much as it did all those years ago.

If I had heard of a spreadsheet in those days I would have used one. Word just spread by magic, it was like a 1970's instagram page and word travelled quickly . We didn't need social media, these trips would normally start with a few of us and had grown by the time we were on the way. It was common to meet at the Students Union first, I never understood how everybody appeared on time, some form of alcoholic telepathy I suppose. A number of variables we had to consider about these events: pubs had a) closing time in the afternoons b) very limited hours on a Sunday and c) shut at 10.30, so these escapades had to be carefully planned. Also these were the days of no mobiles and no one could find out what you were up to, (deep joy). The timings had to include that fallow period in the afternoon when pubs were shut and what did we do then? This had the makings of a 'Bermuda Triangle' trip, i.e when you were in it you were lost forever…

For some reason these trips usually started on a Wednesday/Thursday and I at times may not resurface until Friday/ Saturday, Sunday at the latest. At the beginning of the term , no one told me that a grant was supposed to last all term, for me it was usually a week at the most, then the bank of dad, saying text books were much more expensive than I thought . My favourite route was what became known as route 1, the Union in Dumfries Place , Pig and Whistle, Taff Vale across the road to the Park Vaults which had the best juke box in town, then it depended on time, quick call in the Rummer, up to the Bluebell / Albert cross the road to the Griffin/Philarmonic, then decision time, again depending on times, down the Docks to see Vic or the Icon Jazzmen if they were on at the Quebec, back to Caroline St, for curry and chips. I was a bouncer in Monty's for some time, so go there, get some money, depending the amount, into Qui Quis for cheap sweet cider sold as champagne or Greco's for the biggest T bone I ever saw, usually to sleep on, and eventually home. I had a few calling places by then but they will stay with me for now.

This particular trip was for one of the rugby boys birthday, I chose a route 2 which had the fatal addition of the Old Arcade thrown in. We started well enough Union, Pig and Whistle, Taff Vale and Park Vaults, with afternoon closing, timing was of the essence, these guys wanted to do the Old Arcade as well, so we stopped after Park Vaults and we split to meet at opening time at the Arcade in the late afternoon, I usually went to the Market for faggots and peas , upstairs and annoy the budgies or flick through the records at Kelly's then a sleep wherever.

On the first part of this trip, I knew most by then, but there was one guy lagging behind who I had never seen before which was unusual, as this particular gang of reprobates were well known and he didn't look that he was particularly enjoying himself. I went back to walk with him just to have a chat, he said he had come to college late, his name was Alun, he wasn't anti social as such, but instinct told me he was hiding something. I had a general chit chat, where he was from etc, I remember he was a Valleys boy, but can't remember which course he was on. But it was his call and if he wanted to talk I was always around. This particular group of boys and girls did like a sing on their travels, and the Arcade was usually up for this. We rarely made it before afternoon closing, so it had to be break time, to reconvene as soon as they were open late afternoon. I even asked Alun if he wanted to come with me to the market and tea and just take in the market for a while, he thanked me but said he preferred to stay on his own, then he went and to be honest I assumed he had gone home and was not coming back.

A brief aside about the market, I had been to many markets, there were regular markets in different Valley towns and I used to love just wandering through the bric a brac looking for a bargain. To be honest I still do, although I can afford decent clothes, I love to wander around charity shops, knowing that in the middle of all that crap, there was a little gem hidden away. I've bought most of my suits, jackets and trousers from these places throughout the years and even when I become a multi millionaire world renowned writer (!) I will still be rifling through old clothes at the back of another charity shop. As ever I digress, Cardiff Market was a whole different experience, we all remember places etc. I had looked up the history of the market, close to the current entrance were the Cardiff Gallows, where they hanged the Welsh Martyr, Dic Penderyn in 1831 and the current market opened in 1891. In the early days you had the first Marks and Spencer penny bazaar, and Ashton's Fish counter which started there in the early 1900's. I don't remember after all these years the stalls particularly, but the amazing smells of cooked meats, cheeses, breakfast, mugs of tea I do, and it was always busy. I could spend all day just wandering around, upstairs to Kelly's Records, with the worst statue of Elvis ever seen and endless stalls with budgies in cages and the noise was relentless, but I took it all in . Just looking over the ledge at the maelstrom of every kind of stall imaginable. I loved it then, and it will always be an integral part of my Cardiff .

Anyway back to the story. They all made it back to the Arcade for opening and the singing started big time, there were some good singers and the atmosphere was electric. To my surprise Alun had come back, he was on his own, he was drinking a bit, said he was OK, and I left him. Sometime later when singing was in full flow, he asked me for a quick chat outside, when we got outside he told me the story. His Dad had been killed in an accident fairly recently, he didn't specify how and I wasn't going to pry, and this was the first time he had been out from his home and why he was late coming to college.

I usually have plenty to say, but was not sure what to do here, just told him to stay with it and enjoy as best he could, we went back indoors and it was rocking, guys on tables and chairs singing their hearts out. A tap on my shoulder, Alun, asking if he could sing a song that his dad liked. I said sure, got up on the table and told all that Alun wanted to sing a song, didn't tell them why, eventually it quietened down and Alan got on a chair. Within a few minutes you could hear a pin drop, he sang the most beautiful version of Myfanwy I have ever heard then or since, I have to admit I had tears streaming down my face, and others were the same.

He finished and there was nothing to say, complete silence in a packed Old Arcade. He said goodbye to me, thanked me , walked out of the pub and despite me trying to follow him, he disappeared into the scrum of the city centre. I tried to find him but with no success, not sure if he just needed to do this and move on, or whether he stayed in College but to my regret I never saw him again. After that the other guys were back on it big time but I have to be honest my heart was not into the rest of the night. I left and walked home slowly as reflective as I had ever been, and went to bed thinking of what he must have gone through, and how I would have reacted in the same situation. I was as close to my dad as anyone, and it was hard enough when he passed years later, but would I have had the bottle to do what Alun did? Thank God I never had to find out...

When I decided to write this book, I didn't want it to seem just a tale of drinking, womanising and parties. I did and still do, have an awareness of others and would always look out for people who were struggling for some reason, I heard as many sad tales as I did funny stories and that is why my time in Cardiff was so special, I touched love rarely, Lily was maybe the only one for a long time, my other love was this City, dirty streets, noisy pubs, seedy clubs, alcoholics and prostitution included. Nostalgia is not always about everything was better in the old days, but love things as they are. One of my themes in this book is life is a series of 'what if's' where there are times you have choices and for good or bad you make a decision. It may turn out the best decision you ever made or the biggest disaster, but unless you try you will never know.

The next Chapter is about Lily and is a great example of the 'what if' we have all faced at sometime in our lives.

CHAPTER 7

LILY

To explain my relationship with Lily you have to go back to my early upbringing. I lived in a happy and loving household with my sister who is 6 years younger than me and still lives in the Cardiff area. Being brought up in the Valleys and being the local policeman's son was something I had to learn to live with. We seemed to move quite regularly, as I mentioned previously, I would come home from school to be told we were moving to X, Y or Z next week. I went to too many primary schools for me to remember, made friends for a bit, then moved on to the next one without looking back. As I got older it became for me more of an issue, especially when girls started to appear on to my horizon .

I recall going to a girl's house, Anne , and going to see her and her mum, and when I went in I heard a gossip between her mum and neighbour saying that Anne was seeing the ' Policeman's son' and how she felt that was a good thing, I wasn't 'Howard' or a 'nice guy' but just the Policeman's son. The issue of did they like me as Howard who was a nice guy, or someone who was the Policeman's son stayed with me until I went to Cardiff in 1970. There you were just another student in the eclectic mix of different, races, colours and creeds, none of these issues of colour and race mattered to me even from those early days. I had read and learned about the race riots in the US after the assassination of Martin Luther King in 1968, and somehow instinctively I was appalled. Because of music I used to tune into crackly American radio stations and the differences of perception, depending which part of the US you were from was marked. No wonder Bob Dylan wrote at that time. Just before I went to Uni in 1970 were the killings in Kent State

University of anti Vietnam war demonstrators, to me it just showed the weakneses in American society even then, and if I am honest I have never been a great lover of American culture ever since. Add to that the apartheid in South Africa and the world at my young age seemed a flawed place....

Anyway back to Cardiff. I was to some extent a social animal but on reflection perhaps I wanted to perpetuate that image, but most of the time in that early period especially, I liked being alone with my thoughts. So when I was able to walk again properly, I often went out on my own to go wherever I wanted .

I was in town, I think I'd been to Monty's and rolled into Qui Qui's and there was a group of girls in there, obviously having a great time, one stood out , mainly because she was taller than every other woman and the fact that she was telling the barman their ' champagne was shit' was endearing me to her (also it was).

I glanced at her and thought 'nothing ventured, nothing gained' and asked her would she like a drink. She looked at me and said yes, she would love a double Southern Comfort, I thought Jesus, I have enough for a few beers, but I scraped the money together and paid and she came across and stood with me.

We started talking and I gathered she was from New York and was on an exchange course related to journalism and lived in a flat with a few other girls doing the same sort of thing. How do I describe Lily? She looked like the model, Naomi Campbell, legs up to her neck, black as black, slim and drop dead beautiful... My insecurities were there still, but had now changed from being the Policeman's son to what was a girl like her going to see in a boy from the Valleys like me, but she did, and at the end of the night I asked to take her home and we carried on talking . We stopped outside her flat, not far from where I lived, she grabbed me and kissed me like I had never been kissed before and said something like , 'You're OK and you'll do'. At that point I walked home not sure what had just happened. This was very early in my

Cardiff days, and I didn't know too many people then and this was before many other people were going to come into my life in later college years.

For the next period of my life we were inseparable almost joined at the hip, she needed me, I needed her. We often talked and talked until early morning , she was the first person I had told about my background and the chronic insecurities I had , but it also dawned on me that she had as many insecurities as me for vastly different reasons. I honestly never saw her as black, she was just Lily, she was a good 4 years older than me and it showed that behind her confident façade was a damaged individual.

I knew her better than my new housemates, and I tended not to take her home, but a few saw me with her, and they would say was I knocking round with 'that black girl' which in itself was racist and as I mentioned previously I had this hatred of all prejudice, but especially racial issues, she was just precious Lily to me who cried, laughed, screamed , loved passionately ,and drank with the best. As a naïve 18 year old I was feeling differently than I had ever felt before, Was it love??

We would inevitably always go out together, she was always getting chatted up, but would always look at me and wink and blow a kiss as if to say 'don't worry I'm yours', it was the happiest I had ever been in my short life. On the face of it this relationship looked impossible, firstly she was about 4 years older than me, in your 50's and 60's 4 years is nothing but when you are 18 and her 22 that is a big difference, how far apart were our backgrounds? When she was 18, she was a black woman living in Queens, New York, in a city rife with racial tension as most of America was in the late 60's early 70's, I was 14 living with Mam and Dad in the Valleys, can't even remember where, but on the cusp of coming through puberty and girls now were starting to be of interest.

I felt from the very start this wasn't going to last long, and I wondered then was it worth carrying on. I'm so glad it did. After her time was over in Cardiff she was going back to New

York to carry on her studies . I met her early in October 70, and she was supposed to go back in about the February of 71…

She was breathtakingly beautiful and I felt I was punching far above my weight. I was OK, but I felt she was in a different league to me, but something clicked between us and we just understood each other often without saying anything, perhaps we were the same, both outwardly full of confidence, but underneath some deep underlying insecurities. It really didn't matter why.

My initial plan going to Uni was to go out with as many girls as possible, play the field and worry about relationships some time in the future, Lily changed all that, the only thing going through my body at 18, apart from Brains SA, was buckets of testosterone..but for all the time I was with her I never even thought about anyone else and to be fair neither did she, trust at that level was unusual at that age and time.

Wherever she went she stood out and was propositioned endlessly but she never, ever went with anyone else, nothing was ever said, it was just an unwritten agreement between us..

She was independent, opinionated, clever, sassy, told people what she thought, she had no filters, and you knew where you were with her.

At 18 you have no real idea what love is, as there is little to compare, it was not just physical , it was just a natural progression of our relationship. She had to go to college most days and I didn't, so most of our time was the evening and weekends, but we were inevitably together and as I have said before I was asked was I 'knocking around with that black girl' and I would take off and really go for those who would ask me that.

We argued, disagreed, shouted, would not talk for maybe 5 minutes, I taught her the word 'Cwtch' and she in the end would say to me give me a Cwtch in a real New York accent!!. She was a hugger and a kisser, and many people who were more reserved than her were taken aback, but this was just Lily.

Teo, Walt and many others fell under her spell. I was gone hook , line and sinker, and I was dreading her going. She stayed in Cardiff for Christmas 70, I didn't want to go home but my mother insisted I should go back , I wanted to show Lily off, but my mother's last words to me were, 'I don't mind who you bring back as long as she is not' Coloured, Catholic or Jewish'. It was just the way the Valleys were at the time, as in fairness to her there were few people of other races living there, and she had no contact with anyone. My Dad was a bit more worldly wise. My image of Lily walking through the door of Pontardawe Police station, grabbing and kissing my mam was something that would have caused her a heart attack, my dad was a different character, he would have loved her (he met her once in Cardiff).

I had a miserable Christmas, my sister was only 12 at the time, so she could not help me then, I told my Dad about her and his words were 'you must do what you feel is right boy' I loved him more for that.

I went back to Cardiff as quick as I could, went round to Lily's, and she was there, the look on her face when I walked through the door I will never forget, she hugged me until I couldn't breathe and her flat mates were telling me what a miserable cow she had been!!

Time was moving on she had a date to go back about early February 1971. All I recall now is walking with her to the station where she was getting a train to London and flying from Heathrow, I remember it was bitterly cold and we sat in the Red Dragon Bar in Cardiff Station waiting for her train. For the first time in our relationship her and I both didn't know what to say .The silence was deafening.

In the end a train came, they were every hour or so, and she said 'I need to talk to you before I go', I knew her well enough to have a good idea what was coming so we let that train go. She took a deep breath and said why don't I come to New York with her, the University she was attached to would help me get in and she had her own flat. She had spoken to the College and they would have considered me .

This is not a Mills and Boons novel where I rushed home, picked up my passport and disappeared hand in hand into the sunset. It was one of those heart and head moments we all have in our life. I thought about how much sacrifice my parents had put in to get me to uni, the hurt and distress it would cause them and even the logistics of visas , money etc. In reality she knew, and I did, that it would not happen. And I was only 18 .The next train came in, I looked at her, kissed her goodbye, tears were now falling from both of us. I really had no idea what to do , I couldn't just stand there and wave at the train pulling away . I just turned around and walked out of the station and never heard of or spoke to her again.

I cried and cried , walked to Walt's, (who you will meet soon) hugged him and his Mum, and sat there for a while, pulled myself together a bit and then just walked straight home , no bars etc , went into the house, went to my room and cried for about 2 days solid and then said 'OK, life goes on' and it did....

Over the years, I have loved in many different ways. I married , divorced, and met Suzy and we have been happy for 20 years, she knows about Lily as I have no secrets from her. Love comes at many different levels though. Other friends I have loved at a different level and long may that continue.

Back to Lily. With Social Media and the way communications are now I probably could track her down , but why? She would be 73 now and all I want in my head is that amazing lady I met 50 years ago who had a fundamental affect on my growing up...do I think about her at times?. Yes I do. Do I think 'what if?' Yes I do. Do I think about what she did, kids, marriage etc? Yes I do. Going back to the beginning of this piece when I outlined my hatred of racial issues and the reasons why, it was just coincidence I met Lily then. I wasn't looking for some poor black girl to save, Lily was too independent for that and was a strong willed woman, but at least I learnt first hand what it was like to be black in America in those days. Does it still exist in the USA or even here today? Unfortunately yes, and it is the role of my generation to do something about it, my own children have similar views to me, and they will pass on to my grandchildren and then there may be some true equality in this world. You may sense this is a passionate issue for me and for that I make no apologies. But Lily was just Lily and I am so glad she was part of my life even for such a short , fleeting time.

This has been incredibly difficult chapter to write. Are there any pictures? No, I didn't even have a camera in those days, but the images in my head you can never take away. The theme of this book is that life is a series of 'what if's 'and that short experience I will treasure until I take my last breath. You will not be surprised to know that she pops up frequently during this journey of mine I had almost put her in the back of my mind, but in the writing of this book, she came back to the front of my thinking, and an odd glisten in my eye, happened more than once.

Time to move on to Walt, another of those I met in my early years who was important for different reasons....

CHAPTER 8

WALT

In my trips to the docks area and the Butetown area in the 70's , I was amazed at the number of different religions, castes, and colours which gave that area it's truly unique feel which in my short life I had never experienced before. On my travels, the smells , noises, and just feel of the whole area was a complete fascination for me. I knew nothing of the different types of religion and what they meant. I was, and am still not particularly religious myself but respect those who are. I knew a guy who I met early in my college days who was a Sikh as he wore a distinctive turban. I met him a few times in the union and over dinner one day I made a point of sitting with him. He was doing something scientific, and was aiming to be a chemist of some sort. He was born and brought up in Cardiff, and had a great Cardiff accent!! He must have been second generation, as his parents were pushing him to study, study , study, and get to the top.

I would be a fool to believe that racism was not around at that time, although in my world I didn't see it and would have had something to say if I had. He was a really friendly lad, had a bit of an eye for the ladies, saw him on more than one occasion having a sly glance at Lily, who typically would greet him by giving him a hug, if his skin had been a different hue I would have sworn he was blushing. Like you do, I asked his name, it was something I could not pronounce followed by Singh, so to me he became Walt, as in Walt Singh Matilda… sad I know, but he saw the funny side of it as well.

Natural curiosity made me ask him about his religion, truth be told, he knew the theory, but like many second generation young people he did not have the same commitment as his parents who were apparently very devout. He was a good looking lad, tall slim, looked like one of those Bollywood actors, and you could almost sense the problem he had, follow the religion or go his own way. Instinctively he supported his parents' view but I felt he was not entirely convinced, I being who I was, wanted him to see what else was out there.

I asked him if he drank, apparently under the religion you are not supposed to but many of the Sikh lads did, although he did tell me he had tried it and didn't really like it, but it gave me a gap to exploit the truth of that.

Anyway, we met now and again and out of the blue, one day he invited me to his parents' house for a meal, Lily was with me and she decided she was coming as well, you didn't argue with her and he saw that. I didn't know whether to take a bottle or something or flowers. Lily wanted to take a bottle of Southern Comfort which even I realised was not her finest idea.

They lived down the Bute, I can't remember the actual street, but it was close to the Mount Stuart, which he told me he had never been to, I glanced at Lily and winked, she knew what was coming and poor unsuspecting Walt was in for a treat..!

When I asked the simple question , 'did he eat meat' the answer again was complicated, basically the ultra religious Sikhs did not eat meat or eggs, but others who may not be so religious did, the main premise was that Sikhs should not over indulge in anything. He did explain the foundations of the religion, and I certainly took to the concept of Karma, things have a habit of coming back and biting you on the bum!!, I think his parents largely didn't eat meat , but he said they would make a meat dish just for me, I said no, I will just eat what you do.

I had not met many Indian people before, I had played with and against a number of Indian cricketers, a game in which they were, and still are, one of the world's top sides .I subsequently met a number of Indian people through work in Cardiff many who became friends over the years.

All I can recall here was the overwhelming welcome we had in their house. Walt's parents were both absolutely delightful people. I believe they ran a small shop in the area, but Dad had some health issues and one of their other sons had taken it over. I recall in the small but friendly house a huge vat of curry in the middle of the table, grandma, continually adding stuff and stirring, people popping in and out all the time, helping themselves to some curry, whole families, some obviously from the docks area or worked on the buses, Walt had to translate. Sitting on the floor, cross legged, with no plate, was something I hadn't done often eating in the local bars of Caerphilly...

Now dear reader, my experience of curry at that time was a bit of a Vesta packet and some bland curry in a new place in Woodville rd, mild meat Curry (with the meat not actually specified) half and half, rice and chips, Lily was acting worldly wise saying she had eaten curry in New York etc, but nothing, nothing prepared me for the taste.

Firstly I was looking for a knife, fork and plate, till I watched them just put a chapati in it, and just eat it like that, just as well I wore a, trendy at the time, tie die shirt as more of this curry was on my shirt than went in my mouth. After about 2 bites I lost all feeling in my mouth, they could have ripped my teeth out with pliers and I wouldn't have noticed it, even Lily was almost crying next to me and could not speak. I asked for water and drank about 10 gallons, Jees, I had never tasted anything like it, Walt, the bugger, had this smirk on his lips, he knew and had told his mother that we liked hot food and to add more spices.

I bought some flowers (I lied I nicked them out of a churchyard) and they were delighted , the most beautiful family I had ever met. To mum and dad the family were everything, and that was obvious in the way they looked at their children. I knew it was time to go when mum, through

Walt, asked Lily when we were having children…. I grabbed her arm and disappeared before she said anything..

Dear reader this story does not end here, I asked Walt did he want to go for a quick drink in the Mount Stuart as a thank you, as I explained we had a fantastic time with his parents and extended family there, the colour of the Saris of the women was amazing, and even Lily said she felt underdressed there!! I really should not call him Walt, but he did not mind and to this day I can't remember his proper name. At his home I just referred to him as 'their son' this and that ,which might have seemed strange to them, that was working well till Lily piped in and called him Walt and a puzzled look appeared on their faces, I blagged us out of that somehow. As I said I offered to take him for a thank you drink to the Mount Stuart, he was a bit reluctant at first, but I promised his parents' to look after him. (Lie number 1) and that I would get him home safely in an hour or so (Lie number 2).

It must have been earlyish evening as the pubs and the Mount Stuart had not been open long. In we went , a 6 foot New Yorker with legs that went on for ever, a fairly tall Sikh in his special colourful 'going out' Turban and a 6' 3'' foot Welshman who had more of his dinner on his shirt than he had eaten. My mouth was starting to have some feeling back by now and by not drinking at their house , I had a thirst coming on, as did Lily. I ordered a pint of SA which is all I drank in those days. We had been there before and at least we were on nodding terms with the landlord. He may not have remembered me but Lily you would never forget, and he had Southern Comfort . Walt asked me for the mildest beer as he had not drank much before so I said that SA stood for smooth ale, (Lie number 3) and he would be fine with that, and he said he would have a small one. I explained skull attack to him a lot later on. OK no worries to this point

Then Lily said she was meeting some of her girlfriends at Qui Qui's and did we want to come along, I said we would come for a few minutes (Lie number 4). He seemed to take a shine to SA, so I bought him a pint as they had run out of half pint glasses (Lie number 5) .We had a few and started on our merry way to town, then I said I had to meet someone quickly in the Terminus (Lie number 6) had a couple there, now it was familiar territory, Walt was starting to look happy with SA coursing through his veins, and his turban starting to look a bit wonky, Called in the Philharmonic to pick up a book that a friend was going to leave for me (Lie number 7) a few there and then dear reader the twinkling lights of Monty's reared its ugly head. I said to Walt this was a special private club, which I was lucky to be a member of (Lie number 8), he had never been anywhere like it. Here Lily left us to go to Qui Qui's, so it was just him and I , Monty was there in his dapper waistcoat and little moustache, I had started working there now and he thought I was there to work, but I couldn't leave Walt who was now beginning to sway a little and I was responsible for him.

He was now rocking and rolling and (eventually) we went to Qui Quis and there was Lily with her flat mates, who I have to say were a good looking crowd of girls. Lily hugged me and then Walt as did the others who I knew, who did the same to Walt, he had a smile on his face that never left him the whole night, along with his wonky turban!!

Suffice to say after cheap Cava, passing as Champagne, which Lily hated, Walt was out of it, again I was responsible for him. I ,as always, had run out of money , so Lily lent (gave) me enough to get a taxi back to his home, I bundled him in a cab, singing some sort of rambling Punjabi mantra, I was beginning to feel it as well, anyway we got close to where he lived, and I paid and got him out of the cab. He could barely walk, he had to stop for a pee in an alleyway and one of the street girls whose patch it was, was less than impressed

However I did get him home , basically by now a jibbering wreck, got him to the front door of his house, rang the bell and being the brave man I was ,ran away as fast as I could and hid behind something. All I remember was the door opening and Walt just crashing on the floor in front of his dad and I felt a not too happy pair of parents giving him some grief .

I was worried to be honest , I liked him as did Lily, and I wanted to stay friends, no way to contact him, no phone, no name and can't remember his address.

I was supposed to meet Lily then instead I went straight home, and slept , I have to say uneasily. A few days later I was in the union and I was on my own having something to eat and in front of me plonks Walt. I started to apologise etc, he stopped me and said yes he had had a Punjabi bollocking from his parents but he was so drunk he could not remember, but they were not too bad in the end, basically he said he had a great time as everyone he met just treated him as an ordinary bloke and not the Indian guy with a turban, like Lily was never the black girl from the USA, he was just Walt and Lily was well, just Lily.

We became great friends , I went round there many times, he was the first person I went to see when Lily left, he developed a soft spot in the end for one of Lily's flat mates and they became an item for some time.

I was working out quickly that everything happens for a reason, just be nice to people what or whoever they are and nice things will happen to you. I understood , because of Walt, what Karma meant not only then, but for the rest of my life....thank you Walt.

All the people I met in these early days seemed to be interesting and 'different' individuals, but in the middle of all this ,I met plenty of others, who were fine to be with, but didn't leave the same lasting impression on me. This brings me on to Teo, now him I did remember!!

CHAPTER 9

TEO

I have not mentioned a great deal about my housemates. At the end of year 1 some left and some arrived. We were an eclectic group of reprobates, some with a better attitude to work than I had developed, especially some of the scientists, who had to go to lectures and actually work in college. The 2nd year saw an influx of musicians which made our house a beacon for many as the endless parties witnessed. I will tell you about the day of the alcoholic jelly soon. There was Adrian, who will deserve a chapter on his own, but this is about Teo the Turk..

Teo just appeared one day, he looked like a Turkish version of Charlie Chaplin, short with a moustache and arrived with an unheard of asset, a car........ He wore a tie and jacket and was incredibly polite, as with many, we knew little of where people came from or what they did. All I could surmise was he had come from London to Cardiff, to do what I had no idea.

As many of you at that time, cooking meals was not part of the agenda, fish and chips, burgers outside some club or pub or eating in the Union. It was not a priority, it filled you up between drinking, apart from Adrian whose total diet consisted of Guinness and the odd sandwich. Indian and Chinese takeaways were not really popular then, and a night out in the Woodville was a scotch egg, bag of crisps (remember the salt in those little packets) and beer. We did try breakfast which consisted of whatever was left over from last night and milk which had probably been fresh at some time.

I digress, so Teo arrived complete with a bag of pots and pans, which he started to put out on that thing in the corner of the room, ah yes an oven, we never used it . He then pulled out a pile of spices and things we had never seen or smelt before.

Basically the vast majority of his day was spent cooking some weird and wonderful concoctions, which smelt like nothing I had ever had before. It wouldn't go down well with my mum who was strictly meat and 2 veg, she would not allow this ' foreign muck' in the house, even a packet of Vesta curry was the food of the devil. My Dad loved spicy foods and I recall only once, him and I going for a Chinese in Cardiff, he loved it but I was under threat never to tell my Mum, 10 pints of Guinness was fine, but curry no.

Teo was if nothing else ,a generous guy and he used to cook these huge pots of whatever it was and leave it all day, and was happy for us to partake, understandably we did give it a bashing especially post night out.

He was a little older than most of us and we did try to involve him in the house, he was worth knowing as he had a car and somehow some money and was happy to drive us around. As far as we knew he didn't drink, but a night out with me in the Bermuda Triangle put paid to that....

He was from Turkey and hadn't been in the UK for long. Later we found out his Dad was a big noise in the Turkish Embassy in London, but an innocent question ' where did you do your driving test' was answered with a blank look and 'what is this driving test you mention?' Basically he didn't need one in Turkey and his dad had just got him this car, he had driven through London to Cardiff , never having sat a test... I carried on , he knew nothing of car insurance,or a UK driving licence. So there we were driving around Cardiff with a Turk, in a car which was a rust bucket to say the least with no driving test ,MOT, licence or insurance.

He was a nice guy though and I invited him out one night, I was still with Lily, and I can't remember who else. Off we strolled down route 1, which avoided the Old Arcade, so Pig and Whistle, Taff Vale and it was a Quebec night so off we strolled, we went in ,I think The Mount Stuart. Up to then he was drinking coke, but there we met a Greek guy, again pleasant but I convinced Teo to have a try of the local drink called SA, he took a shine to it and a Turkish version of 'Men's Downhill' was starting but I did not think it was fair to hit him too hard (yet) so he drank slowly.

The Greek guy said to come with him to ' his club' which turned out to be the North Star. Now I hadn't been there before through reputation, and although I was ok in most pubs this was making me a bit twitchy… but in we went , it was dark and smelt of god knows what. It was like a first line of a bad joke ' A 6ft, black American girl, a 5ft nothing Turk who looked like Charlie Chaplin without a cane, a fairly drunk Welshman and a swarthy Greek who looked straight out of Zorbas Dance walked into a pub' all it needed was Walt for a full set… Thankfully the Greek ,who I just called Zorba, he didn't seem to mind, met his mates who were all off a Greek merchant ship with 2 days in Cardiff. I sensed it was not the most comfortable place to stay, they were all looking Lily up and down, and even though she could handle herself, my inherent chivalry decided it was best to go, which thankfully we did. We called in a few, can't remember but we were all together (apart from Zorba). Teo was getting slightly worse for wear and it was getting dark, so I thought , best we got to El Greco's quickly for a bite, and straight home.

I must have just turned to talk to Lily, when I turned back, no Teo, I shouted , no answer, God knows where we were, the girls were starting to come out and I genuinely was getting concerned. A drunk 5ft Turk ,on his own down the Bute, with money in his pocket , a few too many beers, and no idea of where he was.

Our concern was growing , because I felt some responsibility for him, I searched the area which in the dark is not that easy, daren't ask the young ladies on the street could they help me, after some time I have to say we gave up, I was still concerned so went home quickly without going to Greco's.

Got home about an hour later, crept in with Lily, heard noises , went into the living room, who is sitting there, you guessed, Teo …with in his words, ' a nice young lady he met coming back'. He had invited her home, she was very quiet by now, my worry was whether she had got any money from him, he was a trusting soul who would have given it to her (money that is) but the young lady saw me and some of the other guys and decided it was best to leave. Teo was fine and had enjoyed his night greatly, and like Walt before him, felt that he was not being judged by his nationality. Whatever the problems of Butetown, which were numerous in the late 60's and early 70's, it still welcomed all colour and creed, as there were countless nationalities living there anyway.

Despite not knowing him long, he was one of us, and you look after your own. That night he never really understood how dangerous the situation he was in, it was not the place to be on your own in the middle of the night and I and Lily were thankful that he was safe, Lily gave him a hug which looked even funnier, her nearly 6 ft and him about 5 ft, I will let your imagination picture the scene ……

I ,and many others, became fond of Teo. He was a gentle soul who caused no one any harm, and was as giving as anyone I had met at that time. We all felt some responsibility for him, he was with us a short while, then one day I got back home, no smell which we had got used to, pots and pans packed, room cleared and no car. In my room on the bed was an envelope basically saying his dad had told him to go back to London ,plus an envelope with 10 pounds to buy the boys a drink. 10 pounds was a fortune and we had a great night raising a glass to one of life's nice guys. I have to say during that time ,most of the people I came across were genuine people, from as wide a range of backgrounds as you could imagine. Cardiff then to me was the kind of City which welcomed all with open arms and my love affair was to carry on for a lot longer.

It was a City with so many levels which I never fully got underneath. I suppose not being born there had something to do with it. The levels I did unearth were fascinating, and left a long lasting impression on me. I have not loved another place so much ever since those heady days.

Next is the journey of the coal and ore from the Valleys to Cardiff which is a significant and important part of Cardiff's history and one that fascinated me then and it is still evolving years later.

If you are trying to find out who you are, then you are moulded by your family. I have been very fortunate that my sister Helen has kept detailed notes and pictures of our family over the years. She has tracked down relatives who are in different parts of the word including the USA. Without her I would never have been able to add these pictures into this book. These are just a fraction of the pictures that she has, but people I talk about, especially my Mum and Dad, I wanted you to be able to put a face to a story. These images are just up to about 1970.

The next book, ' A Welshman abroad' will include more pictures from the later time I lived in Cyprus and Spain with Suzy

This pic is the youngest of me. I was about one. My Dad decided I was not going to have white curls so as soon as I was old enough they came off. Mam washing me in the sink which was common in the early 50s.

My 2nd Birthday with my mother and my maternal grandmother.

Again I was about two with both parents.

Four generations in 1958, so I was six. My Dad, grandfather on my Dad's side, and a fearsome great grandmother who frightened the life out of me!

Parents' wedding – 1950.

A far-flung relative John Shoreland Westcott, who was killed in
Lagos, Nigeria and a pic of my Dad about the same age. The
likeness is uncanny and both were rugby players of note.

George Westcott, JP, MBE and
an ex-Lord Mayor of Manchester.

Mum, me and my sister Helen.

One of my favourites, me and Dad at Porthcawl.

My Great Grandfather in my father's side.

Rare picture of my Maternal Grandfather and Grandmother, she died very young, and this is the only picture of her with a few of my Mum, brother and sisters.

Dad and his Dad. My dad was about 14 then.

Both of them again, many years later, when my Dad was a
policeman in Sandfields.

My Grandmother on my father's side. From a nursing
background.

Dad's Great Great Grandfather and a very young Dad. The
Grandfather died young, so he was close to his Great Grandfather.

Visiting my Grandad who lived in Dorset then. A happy looking
teenager!

With my Grandad in the caravans he rented in Porthcawl. Visiting him meant a compulsory tie!

Dad in the middle, not long after he joined the police force. My sister kept the buttons on that jacket and I have one as a necklace and another as a ring.

A young Mum in her teenage years.

A later pic of me at the Rag Ball in 1972, with my Joe Cool
Zapata moustache and a bow tie which looks as if a large bat had
landed on my neck...

This is at the Scottish trip of 1969 which I talk about in the early chapters. I'm second from the right.

The unbeaten 7's team 1969. I'm left in front row.

An unbeaten season. Petrochemical works behind – 1969.

Another view of the same game, pictures by my dad.

These pictures are pictures of Cardiff in the 1970's by Tony Othen. Many thanks to him for allowing me to use these images.

CHAPTER 10

THE COAL AND IRON JOURNEY TO CARDIFF

When I moved to Cardiff in 1970, one of the areas as you are aware by now I became fascinated was the Docks area of the city. I spent many happy hours wandering around the streets of Butetown and standing by the Pierhead building, imagining what these new people from all over the globe were feeling as they were entering this new and strange land. I realised quickly that the Docks area was in a period of rapid change, speaking to some older residents down there, gave an insight to what the area was like 40/50 years ago, I gained many friends from my frequent visits to pubs, clubs and homes in the area.

It occurred to me when I came to Cardiff that I had seen the development of this trail from the other end, I had worked in the Rhondda valley and lived in other mining areas where the economy was dominated by coal and iron, and was aware of the history of the mines in those areas. I worked in those Valleys at a time when, like the Docks in Cardiff, the world of these often tight communities was changing. The closure of the mines due to seams running out, the new cheaper and cleaner alternative fuel sources, plus the political struggles which came to a head during the 1980's all added to the uncertainty.

There is much written on this issue and endless information available. This is not a history book, but I will relate it to how I saw the situation through my eyes. But to look at the situation in context you need to look at a brief summary of how the industry developed.

The hills and valleys around Merthyr were rich in iron ore, limestone and coal. The key issue was getting this coal from

Merthyr to the docks of Cardiff and onwards to all parts of the globe. There were 4 major works in Merthyr and Iron masters such as the Crawshays held immense power and influence and wanted their 'black gold' transported to the ports quickly .The answer was to build the Glamorganshire canal from Merthyr to Cardiff. It was a remarkable feat of engineering for the time to build this canal which would travel nearly 25 miles, due to land rising and falling , during the journey it required 49 locks, and this was from 1794 when the canal was opened. In 1798 the canal was extended one mile seawards and included a sea lock.

At this time Cardiff had a population of about 4,000 people. Even in 1850 by far the biggest town was Merthyr, and its population was greater than the combined size of Cardiff and Swansea together. The canal meant that the ironworks were now able to transport their finished iron on a single barge, which could carry 24 tons of iron needing just a horse, 1 man and 1 boy. Three round trips to Cardiff could now be completed in 2 weeks, and this huge influx of coal and iron was going to turn Cardiff into the most important port in the world. Now people were needed from all over to deal with this new demand. The Coal exchange and the Pierhead buildings were now more than figureheads, but symbols of the growing prosperity of the City. But the immense power that the Coal and Iron barons held did not necessarily mean that this prosperity was evenly shared. As I mentioned the Crawshays in Merthyr but now the Bute dynasty in Cardiff was increasingly influential.

John Crichton-Stuart, the 2nd Marquess of Bute, was a big influence on Cardiff at this time. He was a wealthy aristocrat and industrialist in Georgian and early Victorian Britain. He developed the coal and iron industries across South Wales and importantly he built the Cardiff docks.

He focused his daily routine around extensive contact with his estate managers, ensuring his rapidly growing wealth and influence was maintained. He initially married Maria but they had no children, and after she died, Bute remarried and his new wife gave birth to Bute's only child, John, in 1847. So the dynasty was then able to continue.

He was a political and religious conservative, but rarely took part in national debates unless his own commercial interests were involved. Early on, Bute realised the vast wealth that lay in the South Wales coalfields and set about commercially exploiting them through local ironmasters and mines. As I mentioned, he constructed the Cardiff docks, so the growing exports of iron and coal significantly increased the value of his lands in the area, so that on his death he left vast wealth to his son.

There followed further generations of the Butes and the later Butes contributed a great deal to the development of the city , including handing over the Castle to the city in the late 1940's . The early Butes developed the city much more for their own ends and as outlined above no doubt it made them incredibly rich. The Irish were initially the biggest group to come to Cardiff after suffering from the potato famine in Ireland in the early 1860's, desperate for any form of work , they suffered more than most, their accommodation in slum housing , ironically called ' Courts' then soul destroying badly paid work, was not a part of Cardiff's heritage to be particularly proud of.

However what the Irish did bring was this immense sense of community . They had to bond together in this difficult environment and areas such as Newtown, called locally ' Little Ireland' grew, and the Irish did, and still do, add a great deal to Cardiff's history and life.

In many ways there was a parallel with the mining communities I was brought up in, hard men, working in a dangerous environment and again developing this bond in difficult circumstances, especially in the demise of these communities in the 70's and 80's.

During the 70's I still lived in Cardiff but worked as a careers officer in the Valleys above Cardiff. My job was to offer careers advice post school. For many boys their path had been set, their grandads, dads, uncles , brothers etc had all been miners or attached to the mining industry, and they accepted the fact that their future was mapped out by working for the NCB. Many I saw , who lived in the area , were only a 30 minute train ride to Cardiff, but had never been to the city. Their life would always be in the Valley where they were born. They would live there , go to the same pubs, marry a local girl, have kids, play rugby or whatever, and stay there till they died. That was the accepted pattern of Valley life, but the closure of the mines in the 70's and 80's was going to change all that…

Back to Cardiff, just after the second world war, demand for coal slumped as other countries developed their own steel industries, trade was also lost to the larger container ports as the extent of world trade increased and by the 1960's coal exports had virtually ceased. In 1978 the East Moors Steelworks for example closed with the loss of over 3,000 jobs.

With the docks inevitably becoming decreasing in importance , my question was what was happening to the people in these communities in Cardiff? It was important for me to know and understand when I arrived in 1970 .Tiger Bay for example, was a local nickname for the general Cardiff Docks area, the evocative phrase deriving from the area's rough and tumble reputation. Merchant seamen arrived in the city from all over the world, only staying for as long as it took to discharge and reload their ships. Consequently many murders and lesser crimes went unsolved and unpunished, the perpetrators having sailed for other ports. Without these merchant seaman what was to happen to the docks area, and the communities who had become an integral part of Cardiff life? By the 70's and 80's, Cardiff Bay had become a neglected wasteland of derelict docks and mudflats. Its population suffered from social exclusion and had above average levels of unemployment. So what of the myriad of nationalities which had made Cardiff one of the first multicultural communities in the UK ?

From the early 1800's to the time of the Second World War, migrants from more than 50 different countries were brought by the growth and influence of the British Empire to work in the coal industry and international trade. Most of the migrants were men from the Arabian Peninsula, the Caribbean, Somalia and West Africa, but people had arrived there from all over Europe and beyond. Migrants lived mostly in Tiger Bay, or Butetown, which lay within the boundaries of Bute Street and the Glamorgan Canal, and between Greek Street and Hodges Row, many of them settling in Cardiff for good, and marrying women from the South Wales Valleys. Despite the once-squalid reputation of the docklands area, it became a thriving multicultural community rich in culture and understanding. I found through my time talking to people that many of its original buildings were demolished in the 1960s and 1970s. The Butetown I saw was a run down area, but with buildings I felt with some form of restoration would again have been an asset to the City. The planners of 1970's Cardiff had different ideas, and knocked it down. I was frustrated as I just saw the back end of the old docklands, and a myriad of knocked down houses and monstrous tower blocks to replace them. Nothing destroys a community like a concrete jungle, living on top of each other and not able to gossip over the fence. To me it did mirror the Valleys, thankfully without the tower blocks, where the geography of the Valleys at least saved them those monstrosities.

The people of the area was split by generation , the older residents remembered, the 'good old days' of the Butetown Community, but in the 70's , the younger people who were now Cardiff born , second and third generation residents, maybe wanted more out of life. The pressures of the outside world you couldn't ignore. Racism was rife everywhere. In my talks with Lily, 1970's America was a hotbed of racism, and you would be naïve to think that it did not exist in Cardiff. On the face of it I saw none, although Cardiff was a split city with the affluent north of Cyncoed, Lisvane ,

Llanishen etc , and the less advantaged, Splott , Grangetown, Butetown areas, and there was a definite feeling of this is your area and that is ours, until that divide is questioned and knocked down like the buildings of the docks are, these problems will still exist.

On a positive note, the people I met, like Walt and many more, still had this sense of community, and a protection of their families, many did not have much, but what they had they would always share and I loved them for it. In some ways I wished I could be transported to the 40's and 50's, even for a short while to see for myself. A photographer I always admired was Bert Hardy, he took many pictures of the docks area in 1950 and 1954 which were his 2 main visits, complex copyright issues does not let me put those pictures of that era in this book. I encourage you to look at his work and see for yourself. Another photographer Tony Othen , took a number of pictures of the area in the 70's and he has kindly allowed me to share those images with you.

My escapades in college might seem like a time of endless sex ,drugs and rock and roll, well apart from the drugs, which were never my scene , but they were not. This book is about reflections of a time which molded my future attitudes and I wanted to share those feelings with you as well. I am not Cardiff born, people who were born and still live there may have a different perception, these are just mine, in a snapshot of time of my life which was significant.

One of my greatest regrets was that I never even had a camera in college, the images I have are all in my head alone, I would have loved pictures of people and places, but hindsight is a wonderful thing....

Music has been a recurring theme in my life and in 1970's Cardiff, I was involved and saw many iconic and local artists which had a lifelong effect on me as I discuss in the next chapter..

CHAPTER 11

MUSIC IN CARDIFF IN THE 1970'S

In my period in Cardiff , the City in the 70's became a centre of some of the best music of the time. All the top bands and artists played there. The Capitol Theatre , The Top Rank, Sophia Gardens, The Students Union, Cory Hall and even some of the smaller clubs such as the Casablanca and Moon, hosted some of the most influential bands of the era. Many people who think of music and Cardiff, mention people such as Shirley Bassey and Shakin' Stevens, yes, they were iconic, but it was more than that.

Cardiff was a musical maelstrom of the greatest delight for me. In my University time which was 1970 to 1973, many great bands were booked at prices you would not believe. And in the later 1970's, about 1975/6 there were the Concerts in the Castle with people like Thin Lizzie, Queen, 10 c c, Status Quo and many, many more.

There was also a vibrant local scene, including a blues guitarist called Vic Parker who played in a pub called the Quebec in the Docks area. I went to see him early in my Cardiff life and I was totally hooked. When I was younger I used to listen in bed to my crackly wireless to the old American Blues men, Lightning Slim, John Lee Hooker, Sonny Terry and Brownie McGhee. When I saw some of these guys on stage in Cardiff I was dumbfounded.

Having come out of the 'pop' sixties, the 70's brought in a much harder edge than I had heard before. I was not a Beatles or Stones man, I came to appreciate the Beatles in later life but the Stones never rocked my boat, the stuff that bands like the Dave Clarke Five, The Tremeloes, The Searchers,The Monkees etc produced was not for me, there were some exceptions , Moody Blues, Pink Floyd, Procol

Harum, Joe Cocker, Yardbirds and Dylan started to come into my orbit. Many we were lucky to get to Cardiff. Having seen videos of Woodstock, I wished I had been there.

Just before my time, on the 23rd November 1967, was one of the most memorable gigs in Cardiff ever, oh how I would have liked to be there. It was held at the Sophia Gardens Pavilion.

The list of artists were: The Move, Jimi Hendrix Experience, Pink Floyd, Amen Corner, The Nice, and the cheapest seats were 7/6!! Two performances at 6.15 and 8.35...

While I lived there the local scene was also vibrant and I found a varied mix of genre of music on my travels, from old American Blues, trad jazz and heavy rock. Wales in national terms was not of great interest to the London scene at that time. That time would come later with such artists as Cerys Matthews, Catatonia and Manic Street Preachers having a much wider influence. Many away from Wales would just see Tom Jones and Shirley Bassey as the main Welsh artists, iconic as they were, there was a vibrant and growing scene under that.

Cardiff bands ,or bands which had a close link to Cardiff, were beginning to come to the fore, Amen Corner, who had a string of hits in the late 60's , early 70's, and perhaps the more influential Budgie ,whose work influenced some of the major rock bands of the time, including Iron Maiden, and Metallica. Dave Edmunds, a Cardiff boy , had some success with Love Sculpture and then on his own, with the worldwide hit 'I hear you Knockin'.

He did put something back into the scene by opening the Rockfield Studios in Monmouth where he encouraged local bands to develop.

The local bands in Cardiff were never going to make a living at that time, often they relied on money chucked into a bucket and free beer!!

That is the background of the Cardiff I came to in the 70's. One of the lads I lived with ,Dave, became heavily involved in booking events at Cardiff in that period and I have used him greatly in putting this chapter together. Some I remember vividly, an American band called Sha Na Na came to Cardiff, a cash only event as many were in those days, but the highlight for me was the one and only Keith Moon, the man was destined to live a short life as he did, as he took excess to the limit and beyond. A chaotic but amazing gig. We had Status Quo in the small lower refectory in Dumfries Place, rocking the place to a standstill for a few shillings..

A couple of gigs I also remember vividly, I did say that I was heavily interested in the black blues music coming out of America at a young age so I was beside myself when we booked a blues tour. It was bitter sweet as they were really old men, who despite their talent, probably had earned little so they had to do these trips to the UK . They didn't know where they were, did what they had to and shuffled on. The highlight for me was Sonny Terry and Brownie Mcghee. Added to their age at the time, was the fact that Sonny Terry was blind and played harmonica and Brownie McGhee had a paralysed right leg and had to sit all the time, I recall Sonny Terry with a smock with endless harmonicas on it.

To me I sat and watched and was totally transfixed, 2 old Delta Blues men, still playing brilliantly, knowing their roles together instinctively. At the end of the night , they were on a bus off to some other college gig which they would never remember.

There was one classic event, Dave who I mentioned here, had nothing to do with this. The background. It was common that local bands would come to the reception at the Union and ask to play for beer money to get experience , this would happen most nights ,whoever was in charge of the Union that night would not even bother to come to the door, or leave a message to say thank you but no.

One night (I knew who was on duty!!) a message came through that there were some people who wanted to play just for practice. The room in question was also used for sporting activities and the message went back they couldn't play because it was booked by the Badminton Club, you are thinking so what?

At this time Paul McCartney had just formed Wings, and they literally were on a bus , going round colleges asking if they could play, so Paul and Linda McCartney and Denny Laine, were sitting in a bus outside the Union in Dumfries Place, being told by the porter that they couldn't play because the room was booked by the Badminton Club !! I bet Macca had never had that problem before!! As you can imagine every other college they turned up to couldn't believe their luck, it hit the press and the guy who made this decision was NOT flavour of the month!!

OK ,Dave came into his own in our Rag Week in 1972. I recall him and I on a train to London to meet a well known promoter of the time, Ed Bicknall. There we were, 2 young lads in the middle of Soho, booking this band and that, pretending that it was just another day. Me , I almost wet myself with excitement..

We came back with bookings for our Rag Week, think around February, plus a pile of free albums and a free lunch in the depths of Soho.

I'm sure many of you who were in Cardiff at that time probably came to some of these gigs. To be fair to Dave we didn't have a shabby line up for the week.

Dave used not just the Union in Dumfries Place . In Cyncoed we had Curved Air, a sold out gig, with the delectable Sonja Kristina , The Average White Band at the Catering College ' Cooks' to most of us , we even booked for the old Glamorgan Polytechnic at Treforest where Quintessence, a typical 60's / early 70's soft rock band. Also in Llandaff were Stone the Crows with an amazing singer called Maggie Bell who was seen as the Scottish Janis Joplin.

In the context of the 70's these guys were not the superstars they were destined to be, but just guys learning their trade. Thin Lizzie, Ralph Mctell, Steeleye Span, Shakin' Stevens and others also crossed our doors.

The highlight of our week was our Breakfast Gig in the Top Rank. Dave had booked Humble Pie, one of those super groups of the time, Vinegar Joe, with the raunchy Elkie Brooks ,and Manfred Manns Earthband. As you can imagine, tickets sold out quickly. Humble Pie with Steve Marriott were big news and were just coming back from an American Tour.

We had many meetings with the Rank, they were slightly nervous about doing deals with a bunch of long haired students and if I recall a fair sized deposit had to be paid.

Anyway, we were going to make a decent profit for our charities for this. I remember being in the Rank when Humble Pie turned up, with God knows how many large trucks of equipment.

They came in , typical 70's divas, and the management looked at the stage said it wasn't big enough to get all their equipment on and they were not going to play.

We were still young lads thinking , oh shit, how are we going to get out of this , a sold out gig with no headline act. Somehow, someone with a quick mind, got hold of a scaffolding company and explained the situation and to their credit they were there quickly, and at some cost, they extended the stage . Problem now was that it had reduced the capacity by quite a lot, anyway we just thought we'll pack them in a bit tighter. Then the equipment came in.....banks and banks of speakers, made Status Quo look like an acoustic group, next thing that worried the Rank Management was would they smash all the glasses behind the bar, I recall Marriott starting to rehearse and it was so loud, even before guitar and drums, I had to sign something saying that we were responsible for any damage and pray that nothing untoward happened.

I remember the stress of the whole thing was starting to get to me and I didn't feel too well, a great deal of pressure for a young lad, and it was the start of a lifelong issue for me. I remember the gig starting Manfred Mann were OK, Vinegar Joe were awesome, Elkie Brooks had that brilliant voice with that rough edge and looked sensational, shame she turned into a ballad singer with no edge. Then dear friends I remember nothing, I must have collapsed and remember waking up in the back of an ambulance, starting to come around, wanted to go back but they kept me in.

Apparently the event was fine and Humble Pie brought the house down, and didn't break any glasses, but I was out of it. Realised, even at that early age, that stress and pressure causes me problems, which has lived with me through most of my adult life. I have developed strategies to deal with it now, but it's still on my shoulder and I have to take care..

Anyway back to music, looking back it was a great time , saw all the top people either in the Union or any of the other venues, especially the Capitol and Sophia Gardens where most of the great musicians played , Elton John, Queen, Who, and many others and those amazing few years in 1975/6 with the Concerts in the Castle ,were awesome. I have a lifelong love of Steeleye Span who I first saw in the Cory Hall and Ralph McTell there as well .The days that Queen, Thin Lizzie, 10cc etc played the Castle the weather was a nightmare, but atmosphere was great Bowie and Michael Jackson also performed in the Arms Park in the 80's, I wasn't there but the Jackson concert lives in the memories of people that went.

But the other side of me was happy on my own, into a local club, especially the Glee Club, The Moon ,and many others with the inevitable bottle of Newcastle Brown or down the Quebec with old time blues with Vic Parker.

They were heady days indeed and you realized why these bands became so good, they learned their skills playing in cramped sweaty students unions and the like for peanuts. In the 70's you could not hide behind electronic wizardry, you were good or you were not, nothing was fabricated and downloaded onto Spotify.

I always loved going to places like Spillers and Kelly's records in Cardiff market to buy LP records, where you had covers you could read, even booklets with them and the words of the songs, they were my pride and joy. I am glad to see this retro market is coming back, trying to buy and fit a new needle for your record player was a delicate operation!! And the crackly sound compared nothing to what it is now, but my collection of records was my pride and joy. Nostalgia is not always ' The good old days' but with music for me it was. I played a bit onstage on my own over the years when I went to Cyprus, that was how I earned my living, playing long gigs at bars and hotels, it did take me back to the 70's. I loved being on stage and I did have a modicum of talent , but that is another of those 'what if' moments we have in life…

I also recall some of the lesser known acts, who had nowhere to stay, coming to stay at our house. A rock and roll pianist called Erroll Dixon, rocked the Union, had nowhere to stay, so he rocked our house as well!! Heady days. Dave reminded me of a time when he wanted to book Adge Cutler and the Worzels, but they were too expensive, so the agency sent us a group called Shag Connors and the Carrot Crunchers , they did 2 or 3 sets in the Union and went down a storm!!

Roll on 12 months and we wanted a German style oompah band, what happened ? , the same group of guys as the year before turned up complete with lederhosen, different instruments and rocked the place again!! They turned up again as a trad jazz band , again with different instruments and again rocked up a storm.

Dave was sure if we had asked them to turn up as a skiffle or a country and western group, they would have. They didn't charge a lot and were just great musicians who did everyday jobs who were having a ball.

Oh great days…OK on to a brief introduction to my housemates and the saga of the dismantled bed…read on.

CHAPTER 12

HOUSEMATES

It is slightly confusing still to me who was there in the first and second years, I was lucky to get into a student house early because of my injury, however it was the second year was when it really took off, …. A number who I am still in touch with. John M who became a renowned Microbiologist in Canada, he has come to Spain for a meet up . John R, who was from North Wales, singer, raconteur. John L, again Wales, great guitarist who played in various bands. John H, who I never got to know really well. Keith W, who became a book publisher in Scotland. Dave S who was from Manchester, another musician, ended up in IT in London and singing with the London Welsh Male voice choir. Dave R, from Liverpool area, a fanatic for Tranmere Rovers (someone had to be!!) was best man at his wedding to Karen, they are still happily married living in Gloucester way. The best present I got Dave for his wedding was a signed letter from Tranmere Rovers wishing him all the best for his wedding, sure he still has it!! Nick, my best friend at the time, Manchester, doing accountancy, became an accountant with the Open University, did a few of his weddings and he was best man at my first marriage in Cardiff.

Then there was Adrian, where do I start, he just appeared, mad as a hatter, played piano and drank Guinness, flamboyant, we think gay, but he never bothered any of us, spent his day (and night) playing and drinking, a phenomenal, flawed talent, apparently studying music but never seemed to go to college. He had one of the two single rooms in the house which was best , which he turned into something else, silver foil on the walls, black everywhere, and interesting smells which stretched through the house…If you asked him to play 'three blind mice' for example , you would throw at him a name and he would play it in that style, amazing.

He had a lot of visitors, the first I recall was, a men's hairdresser, who all I remember was that he had flowers tattooed all over his arms and clothes, think he was called Justin, he did not last long, we would support him through these tragedies until the next one came along.. then one night, the bell rang and at the door was a sight none of us will forget, must have been a 6 foot bloke, who needed a shave, but dressed as a woman complete with makeup, long sparkly dress, hand bag, high heeled shoes, who answered to the name of Claudia.Up he went to Adrian's room to be there forever... Truth be told we all became fond of Claudia, he was often around and he became part of the furniture, we did not care what Adrian's sexual orientation was, the deal was he never tried anything with us, which he never did, and he was an integral part of our little community, we occasionally took him and Claudia on one of our many pub visits, and they were often subject to typical homophobic comments, but he was one of us, and upset them and you answered to all of us.

I have to say however , I avoided taking him on my often solitary docks sojourns, as I would have worried in some of the pubs down there.

The place was a haven for musicians, I played guitar and honed my skills with some great players there. We became well known, for some reasons student nurses loved it there and if any of you were student nurses in the early 70's you may have been to one of our evenings, they were like bees to a honey pot. Nurses we found worked hard and played hard and we were happy to accommodate them!!We also used to make alcoholic jelly, and home brewed beer , which we assumed was drinkable after a few days, waiting for beer was not one of our strengths, so a glass of brown sludge with lashings of jelly full of cheap red wine was our interpretation of a buffet night.

As I mentioned we only had 2 single rooms, one was Adrian's, which we never went in unless we had a can of Guinness for him. Once we had the piano (and how we got that is a story on its own) he was happy. You would have a blinding hangover, get up early for a drink or pee and he would be bashing out the complete works of Wagner at 6 in the morning and he would shout on the top of his voice ' which one of you darlings has my Guinness'. hey ho.

The other single room was an issue, we were all healthy lads, and any morning there were often various females draped around the place , with one bathroom there was often early morning tension, we had developed this close link with the nurses training college , they spent hours in there.

We were all often desperate to book this room as we all shared, apart from Adrian. One of the more organized housemates had put a booking sheet on the door , where you could book the room by the hour, maximum 2 hours. Girls did ask what the form was for , we normally blagged by saying they were cleaning or shopping rotas.

One lad , let's call him John, had never booked the room before, one night he rushed in and with barely concealed excitement asked if he could book the room, not only that he wanted to book a double session, 4 hours! Unheard of.

There was always one of us who was HOR (Head of Room), unfortunately I was not it this particular week and the holder of the key, who felt sorry for him, let him have it a few days hence. He was duly given the key as there were no other bookings before then.

Now being the boys we were ,we were not going to make this easy, the room itself was small and could fit no more than a small bed with a bit of wiggle room, but it served its purpose.

Poor old John was on tenderhooks, especially on the morning of his date, we did not know this girl. We had arranged between us to make a 'memorable' evening for them. John went out early evening, scrubbed up and ready. Just after he left we went into the room. This room was next to the fire escape which was why it could not be let out properly.

Typical Cardiff summers day it was peeing down which made it better for us. So we stripped the bed at least, then dismantled it piece by piece, passed it through the fire escape and then put it back together and it just about balanced on one of the bigger steps. This took about 4 of us an hour or so, we even put the mattress outside as well, nice guys we were, we at least took the sheets off.

John thought he had the only key, but like you do, we had a few copies cut. Then my friends it was just sit and wait, he was taking her for a meal, if we had known where we would have joined him.

Can't recall the time but the door went and in walked John, with this shy thing behind him, she was nice enough and we should have felt ashamed at what we had done... but we didn't. We were casually talking and he just slipped out of the room and went upstairs.. All I recall was a massive scream BBAAASSSTTTAAARRRDDDSSS!!!

Anyway we expected him to come running down to bollock us, we were surprised that he stayed in the room for the full 4 hours!! He eventually came in , said little but did say he was taking her home.... Natural curiosity saw us piling upstairs, going in and found this soaking mattress had been pulled in, and he must have gone in his room for towels. We were very impressed by his tenacity in this situation, it was never mentioned again and we never saw her again. As you can see very mature times.

We loved winding each other up, you never knew what would happen next or who would do it. One of my contributions was that I came in very late one evening after finishing in Monty's ,to find the place unusually quiet. A lot of the guys did have cereal and stuff for breakfast, and in the cupboards were a bunch of boxes with everyone's name on it. If you have shared a flat or house you will know how possessive people are about their food, all had people's names written on them. What did I do? I got some scissors and carefully cut all the cardboard bottoms off each packet , then cut the inner bag that held the cereal, then put them back as carefully as I could so that when they picked them up the cereal would be everywhere.

I then went to bed , crashed out, and was not up when I heard a great deal of interesting language from the kitchen. I stayed there pretending to be asleep in case they came in and blamed me, by the time I got up they had all gone, apart from Adrian , in some amazing smoking jacket playing the piano. There was cereal and boxes thrown everywhere , 1-0 to me!!

Many of us went on to work in highly responsible and demanding jobs and I'm sure that the creativity we had and our ability to do things under pressure , would make us better people in the future...

....If you believe that bollocks you are as bad as the rest of us !!. Another little escapade was getting a piano in the house, and my own time with Rita, read on...

CHAPTER 13

THE HOUSE PIANO AND RITA

This tale turned out to be one of humour and pathos. As I mentioned when we spoke before, we had gathered a house full of musicians, not only Adrian but a few others, played piano. We decided to keep Adrian out of trouble if nothing else and to get a piano in the house. The problem ? How are going to get a piano with not a lot of money between us, plus how would we get it back to the house, resourceful we were if nothing else. We asked around and I can't honestly remember how , but there was someone who was working in one of the uni offices who joined us for a drink now and then, who thought an old neighbour of his may have one she was not using any more. We asked him to find out and he eventually came back to us and said she was happy to get rid of this old piano if we could take it away.

We found she lived a fair distance away, it was across Wood St Bridge, towards Cowbridge road and somewhere off there, so one weekend a few of us decided to have a stroll and have a look. The danger was we were walking through town, which was thirsty work and after a long walk, with various pubs and pee stops we reached the house .Now picture 4 strapping lads, knocking a door in a backstreet of Cardiff after X pints.. We knocked and eventually a little old lady came to the door, opened it a little bit, and asked who we were , we explained we had come about the piano, she said OK, just opened her door and let us in.

Can you just imagine doing that in today's world ? It just shows how the world has changed, not for the better I'm afraid. But we were all nice genuine lads, we walked in to this small, tiny in fact, house , but neat and tidy and walked into her living room and there on the table was a teapot (complete with hand made cozy) and a plate of cake and biscuits. I could have cried then, emotional bloke I was. She told us her name was Rita, she looked like everybody's favourite granny, gray hair in a bun, neat but faded clothes, thin arms and hands you could almost see through and the compulsory pinny. She asked us to sit down which was difficult as there was one small sofa and a wooden chair and 4 hulking lads, but we managed. She had her own chair which was her territory. Then she offered us tea and biscuits, the tea had been warmed many times but we didn't complain, included the little dish of sugar lumps with those tongs things to pick them up, and she even had put serviettes into napkin rings.

In the corner there was this fairly old upright piano , with plants and pictures all over it. In these situations you look around for pictures of kids, grandkids etc but I saw none. There was one old grainy black and white faded picture from a long time ago of her and obviously her hubby on their wedding day, but it was quickly obvious there was no hubby around but she did refer to 'my Bill' many times.

She wanted to get rid of the piano as it was taking up too much room . 'Her Bill' used to play years ago but it hadn't been played for many years. We had general chit chat and were then going to go home to find a way to get it from her house to Glynrhondda St. I don't know why but I felt she wanted to talk, so I said to the lads , I'll stay for another cup of tea and catch up with them later.

I sat back down and she asked me about college and where I was from etc then I asked her to tell me a bit about her life. About an hour or so later she was still talking and talking. A summary, her husband Bill had died about 6 months previously. He had worked in the parks and gardens department of Cardiff City Council for over 30 years, they had been married for something around 50 years, she must have been around 80, it was hard to tell, so married around 1920's. They had no children ,and that I found later was the issue, she was chronically lonely, she had gone to bingo at one time, but her best friend who gave her a lift had gone away and she couldn't get there. Once Bill had gone she had nobody and she told me we were the first people she had talked to for about 2 weeks. She did go to her local shop for the meagre food she seemed to have.

It was fairly obvious that money was a problem, I even asked how she managed on her pension and Bill must have retired and had a pension, but she got little from the council and did not know how to chase it up to see what the problem was. No phone, no money, no transport and afraid of authority.

Even at that that early stage , I knew that Rita was going to be someone who I could make a difference to, she had come into my life, like Lily, and I was going to make sure that the rest of her days had some meaning to them.

I am not some superhero who leaps into solve everyone problems, but those who came into my world who needed help, I was damn sure I was going to do my best for.

This story has 2 strands, the saga of the piano and Rita.

I left her and said I would see her soon ,and I did. I walked home , no pubs , just thinking of her and what I could do practically to help. When I got home ,I never mentioned Rita and they told me what they had in mind to get the piano... the great minds and intellects had come up with a plan, we were going to build a sort of pull along trolley on wheels with this long handle so that we could sort of pull it through town. Someone who was vaguely practical had a pen and paper and was drawing stuff, this was not my world so I let them get on with it. Anyway the following weekend some of the boys had put this thing together and on a Saturday afternoon off we went, one of the few trips Adrian came on with us. He was a great help, sitting on the back of this thing , drinking his customary Guinness, on a wooden chair, which later on I realised why it was needed.

Rita had insisted she did not want any money, but we had to do something, none of us had much, but Adrian always had something on him, and as the piano was mainly for him, he chipped in a few quid. Between 11 of us we scraped about 12/13 pounds, I put it safely in my back pocket and left it for later, as you can imagine the trip through town took some time with various stops (again) and Adrian at this time asleep on the back of this trolley.

We got to Rita's and she was so pleased to see us all, as for once something different was going on. We carefully cleared the piano, Adrian has a quick go at it, needed tuning, but to us it sounded remarkably OK. It wasn't heavy between us all and to be honest we got it on the trolley quite easily, a few ropes to keep it on and we were ready for off, now the fun started. Before that next bit , I hung back and stuck the money in her hand, she tried to give it back as I knew she would, but I made her take it as I said that the boys would be upset if she gave it back. I had the feeling that for her this was a lot of money and it went into a pot on the shelf. As I left she said any time I wanted a cup of tea to call around any time as she was always in. At that point I was bloody determined to sort the issue of Bill's pension for her. Another day for that.

By the time I got out , the boys had gone, didn't take long to catch them up and the sight of Adrian now sitting on the chair, bashing this piano along the road with great gusto, it had the makings of an interesting trip home, and , ladies and gentlemen, it certainly was…..

Picture this if you will, pulling a makeshift trolley with a piano on it through a busy Cardiff centre , late afternoon on a Saturday. The problem was the guys had drunk a fair bit there, and with the pubs just opening again we had to stop and have one. Adrian was now really into it, sitting there knocking out tunes, a few of the guys who were good singers were now on this trolley when it stopped and impromptu sing songs were starting.

Suffice to say, this meant that people were sticking their head out of the pubs to have a look. Now and then people would join in and decided to come along with us, the deal was you could come as long as you shared the trolley pulling duties. Word had obviously got around and people turned up to watch and listen. Adrian , being a born entertainer, was loving it, then trays of free beer were coming out from landlords who were doing better business than normal as a thank you, now it was fast becoming Ski Sunday, Men's Downhill. As you can imagine progress was slow, one of the guys had rushed home and picked up 2 guitars which a number of us played , so now it was a pianist , 2 guitarists and a few singers, anyway next stop was outside the Philharmonic. Suffice to say, the trolley was like the pied piper and the crowd was now getting bigger and louder, then people were shouting, asking for requests and I said it was so much, can't remember how much, to do requests , then an idea came to me . I had a bag and put the money in it and told people that all the money we would take we were going to give to Charity, and people were putting a fair bit of cash into our bag.

Now we came to a problem, we needed to get through the market, now the market was about to close ,but nothing ventured , nothing gained. As you know the market is quite narrow and people about, but in we went, Adrian and crew still giving it some and still asking for charity money, the bag was beginning to fill. That was the only time we got stopped by the plod, who understandably asked what we were doing.

Taking the piano for a walk was all we could come up with, we just said it was a charity stunt and they shrugged their shoulders, as ever we were not causing anybody any harm, though the market, just, and then the Old Arcade.... That really set the cat amongst the pigeons. They were great, we even managed to get the piano, which by now was not looking its best into the pub and an epic party unfolded.

The landlord had various charity tins on the bar and I asked him for a spare one rather than our flimsy bag. I looked at the charity tins and they were all charities we supported , Tenovus especially and a special school in Gabalfa somewhere.

Free beer was still just appearing, then the odd pie and I said I would be back with a donation, I did.

We wended our weary way, slowly by now, up Queen St, by the time we reached the Taff Vale, Adrian had had enough, he slumped over the piano and the day was over. It was getting late so with one last effort we got back to Glynrhondda st . Got the piano off, carried Adrian to bed, and all of us crashed out. Just so glad it wasn't the days of smartphones...

I had hung on grimly to the now 2 full charity tins we had plus some in the bag. To be honest for me I had not drank too much, so I was up early the following morning.

Took me some time to count the money and I was gobsmacked as it came to nearly 150 pounds which was an enormous sum for the early 70's, Cardiff was an incredibly generous place even then. Never to any of us was there a thought that this money was ours. We had had free beer and food and a great craic.

Had to wait till Monday to take all this shrapnel to change into notes in the bank, there were an amazing amount of pound notes in there as well. I remember the amount clearly, it was 154 pounds and a few pence. As I said I would , I went back to the arcade and the landlord was just clearing up the bar. I think he was surprised to see me but a promise is a promise. He had 4 different charities so I put 25 pounds in to each one, he was chuffed and offered me a beer, and amazingly I said no, as I had things to do.

I had 54 pounds left, I then walked through Cardiff to Rita's , she was pleased to see me, the kettle was on and I sat down. I said what had happened and that because of her piano we had raised a lot of money and this was her share. I had added a bit to make it 60 pounds, and I passed it to her and said ,' before you give it back you have earned it' .

That amount of money was a King's ransom to her, a few tears came, but in the pot it went. The money we gave her before was still there so she had over 70 pounds.

I hadn't finished, I told you about the problems she was having with Bill's pension, and I had spoken to my solicitor friend Simon and I asked him if he could help, and like I expected he readily agreed. All Rita had to do was sign a letter giving them power of attorney to act on her behalf.

In Rita's I pulled this out, explained what we were going to do and all she had to do was sign this letter and we would deal with it. I had worked out that the council were not going deal with a scruffy student but a reputable firm of Cardiff Solicitors was another thing.

She said nothing would happen, and I said that at least we had to try. I had arranged to meet Simon in the Taff Vale which was a bonus anyway, and gave him the signed letter.

True to his word , he was all over the council like a rash, and it turned out there had been an 'administrative error' and that she was not getting the right amount. In fact there was back payment owed of nearly 400 pounds plus his actual pension payments for her were nearly doubled monthly. Simon had asked me did she have a bank account, but like many older people, she just had a post office savings account. I had seen it and she had 9 pounds in there… I had the number and gave it to him and the council had said the money would be transferred within a week.

I went back to Rita's and explained the situation to her, there was disbelief and she didn't know what to say. She croaked a thank you and I just said this is just what you were owed. I said the money should be in her account in the Post office in about a week. Then I left and went home.

Of course I could not get hold of her and left it a while, eventually I went around and a different person answered the door, smiling and less worry lines. The money had come and she had had a letter (The council also had the wrong address) saying how much she was going to get and when.

I asked her what she was going to do with it and she had no idea, I walked with her to the bus station where we got a season ticket for the bus so now she could get to Bingo on her own. The house was hers, but there was a problem with the plumbing, I knew a plumber from Glamorgan Wanderers rugby (a later story..) who fixed it for a few beers. There was a newish community centre near by, so I took her down there and she met the lovely person who ran it, and they did tombola days, tea dances , and, joy for Rita, bingo 4 times a week.

She said she wanted to buy me a present I said I don't need anything, but I might need somewhere to put my head on my boys night out. She a gave me a key to the house and I also went to BT to see if I could get her a land line put in and were there any grants, etc for older vulnerable people, there were, and in a few weeks she had a phone (took me a few hours to show her how it works!!) . She was starting to meet people in the Community Centre and she was back to her beloved bingo.

I told nobody this, this is the first time I have told the full story.

What did this time mean to me,

Loneliness is one of the most soul destroying situations to be in especially if you are older and vulnerable and end up living on your memories. In the last few years I am sure that isolation and chronic loneliness is as big a killer as Covid, this hasn't changed since those times I was talking about, especially if you have lost a soul mate you have had for most of your life.

It happened to me. My Dad died when I was living in Cyprus, got back to Newport to miss his death by a few hours, him and my mum again had been married since just after the war and about 8 months later , my mum died as well. Apart from physical issues, I'm sure she died of a broken heart as well.

I did nothing special, I was just in the right place at the right time for Rita, how many other Rita's are out there? As a society we have a responsibility of care, yes, instinctively I want to help people who need help, as do most, but we need to do it.

The 70's world where I was brought up, especially in the Valleys, and some parts of Cardiff, had the community around them for support. In the isolationist world we live in, there is a danger that we just worry about ourselves, those times did have positive features which today's younger generation could learn from...

P.S I did appreciate Rita's for a place to sleep on certain nights!! I even had my own room....

Postcript.. I stayed in touch, as time went on, by phone, but life was getting busy for her and me . I popped around occasionally for a chat, but she now had a good circle of friends and activities to keep her busy and the house had a had a few repairs and a paint job an more importantly she was happy. She went on till her 90's , I had moved away from Cardiff by then, but a friend of hers who had my number, I was living in the Midlands then, told me she had passed.

I went back to her funeral, there was a good crowd there. How many other people pass away with no one there as Rita would have, and everybody knew of me and I am so glad she lived her final years with some form of happiness. I had helped her do her will and she had decided to sell the house and give the proceeds to the Tenovus charity in Cardiff , which in the past I had suggested. Dear readers, we can all make a difference if we want. Walt's Karma applied as much then as it does now.

This then takes me on the Rag Week I was responsible for, and as ever, there are tales to tell......

CHAPTER 14

RAG WEEK

Somehow, and I can't recall how, I was elected Rag Chairman for 1972. I remember it as it was the first time I had experienced stress and pressure in my life, till that point I only had myself to worry about and look after , could do what I wanted, when I wanted and that suited me, beer, women and general misbehavior was the story of my life.

Suddenly I was Head of what turned out to be a huge affair, with money and responsibility for others, press, publicity, etc which for a still young lad from the Valleys, was a daunting experience. Luckily most of the people around me were friends and I knew them all, without that it would have been impossible to cope.

I am going to focus two particular events The Rag Parade through the Centre of Cardiff with floats made by various students and the Rag Ball in Cardiff Castle. OK the Rag Parade first. This was the first time I had dealings with the police, other than my dad, I was called to a meeting with the Principal of the College, first time I had ever even seen him who basically said that he did not want anything that was going to cause embarrassment to the College, …no pressure then.

We decided some time before the theme for this parade was going to be films, meet in Dumfries place, into Queen Street, down Queen Street, up St Mary street rattling cans, selling Rag Mags etc to make money for our designated charities, I had already been on the radio and the papers and in those days there was a packed street come to watch on a busy Saturday. What could possibly go wrong??? Ohhh lots.

I was warned by the police that the floats should not have anything ' inappropriate' on them, I think our definition of inappropriate was slightly different than theirs however.

The winning float was going to be judged by a number of people on a temporary stage thing, fairly early in Queen Street, they included the Chief of Police, The Principal of the College, and various dignitaries who I can't recall ,but the night before I had been on a pub crawl and had a horrendous hangover...(plus a few early ones to settle the nerves).

So there I am on this dais near the Dumfries Place end of Queen St .I had had a quick look at some of the floats and to be honest most of them were really good, a great deal of effort had gone into many of them and (fatally) I started to relax...

The next bit was up to that time one of the most cringing times of my life .It started well, the first floats came around the corner and they were generally very good, can't remember all the movies, but a great one with a Yellow Brick Road, a Mary Poppins one. Then......

To give you the background , I think a year before a film came out with Welsh actor Hywel Bennett called ' Percy' now the movie was a about a bloke who had an accident and had a penis transplant which he called Percy, can you see what's coming.. ?

This had been hidden away and appeared at the last minute, around the corner came a massive cardboard Penis with 2 massive balls as well... balls, either side was 2 sort of hoists which could move this beast up and down, people started pointing and laughing. I froze and I had to act really quickly ....

The look I had from the Principal and the Head of Police indicated I was not their best friend. I somehow managed to get them to turn out of the main parade and pulled up by the Park Vaults and as quickly as they could, dismantle this thing. (I have to say it was brilliantly made) but at the back I noticed a massive vat of milk, I didn't even want to go down there , just as well I got it off the main strip, imagine if this had gone down Queen St and St Mary St. Luckily it was only in the parade for a short time but can you imagine social media if there were smart phones in those days!!

When I got back on this dais , I just carried on as if nothing had happened, stiff upper lip came into play, all I recall was one of these great and good people had the outline of a smirk…

PS Percy's float didn't win.

That Night there was a Rag Ball in Cardiff Castle Banqueting Hall. Full evening dress with all these people coming, and I had to give a speech to all this lot.

I have very mixed emotions of not having a camera in those days, there are few pictures around, I would have loved some of the haunts I used to frequent, especially the inside of pubs and clubs like Monty's, Quebec etc, but you just have to rely on memories. The Rag Ball was an event that again adds another piece of the jigsaw that makes me who I am.

After the Rag Parade, which despite Percy, went well and raised a great deal of cash, amazingly I have a copy of the Rag Mag of that year, with some of the worst 'jokes' ever put on paper, done by a crowd of us in the union bar one night. I also have a picture of me dressed up in my finest ,plus a copy of the, typically 70's, menu.

We had decided it was black tie for men, now this was a whole different world for me, all of us trooped off to the local Moss Bros to choose a DJ. The photo I mentioned shows me in my DJ, I really thought I was Joe Cool, but the bow tie looked as if a bloody bat had landed on my neck. I had no idea what you were supposed to do with a cummerbund for God's sake. I could just feel it slipping down my legs from my waist despite the endless safety pins to attempt to keep it in place, so by the end of the night it was around my head like a bandana, lost my Dicky, and poured red wine over my trousers and shirt. Moss Bros were not going to be too happy…..

Anyway the event was daunting, it was a Dinner Dance. I had to give a speech on the top table to about 100 people plus the great and good of Cardiff who I was sitting with. I can't recall who I was sitting next to, she was someone's wife, she sensed my nervousness and tried to put me at ease, she had obviously done this many times before.

I thought about the situation I was in. A lad from the Valleys, about 20 at the time, in a bloody Castle, in a dinner suit, giving a talk for about 20 minutes to the top level of Cardiff society. A few nights before I was rocking and rolling in Monty's, now this.

I had spent days writing notes on what I was going to say, about 20 times a day saying it over and over again in front of a mirror. I was nearly last on, the Principal, Mayor and someone from the charity had all spoken eloquently and it was now my turn. I needed a pee at that exact moment, but I got up, there was complete silence. I looked down at my notes and couldn't see a thing, a few seconds passed, I then just folded my notes put them back in my pocket , took a deep breath ,and decided to talk from the heart about how proud I was of the money that we had raised and how it was going to make a difference etc.

I must have spoken for 15 minutes I suppose and sat down. The clapping started and even the Principal gave me a nod of approval, the sense of achievement was better than the feeling I had after endless beers.

From that moment on my life changed. In my career as it progressed I would often have to speak to conferences, even on one occasion at the Royal Albert Hall which was full. I never had any notes, yes I had prepared what I was going to say in my head, but I just got up and spoke with no nerves or notes. I loved it.

One theme through this book is to talk or write from your heart and say what is in there, emotions and all, people will relate far more. I became popular on the conference circuit and got paid very well. All this happened as a result of that one night in Cardiff Castle. It is one of the occasions that just adds to the rich tapestry of your life, and makes you the person you are.

Thankfully it was many years later I had to speak at my dad's funeral. Emotion wasn't difficult obviously, but he was an incredibly popular man, there were 100's of people from different aspects and times of his life ,and it was in a packed Thornhill crematorium in Cardiff and I had prepared notes, mainly to give to my mother, but again I just talked from my heart in front of all these people and they all knew what I was trying to say. I had a million thoughts I wanted to get across about him but instinctively I mentioned just the things that were dearest to his heart , especially family . I just hope and pray I did him proud.... He and mum, would have been so proud of this book, and deep down it is for them both. In what seemed like just a heartbeat, I had to do the same kind of talk for mum , again at Thornhill, and it took me some time to deal with the situation that I had gone from two parents to none, in a short period of time. It was a great comfort that it brought me and my sister much closer together to share the grief we were obviously both feeling, and that closeness will stay for all of our days.

Back to Cardiff and by now instinctively, I knew this period was coming to an end as the next chapter explains...

CHAPTER 15

BEGINNING OF THE END

As I intimated after the Rag ball, I realised all good things come to an end. The commitment I made as soon as I arrived in Cardiff to give it 100% fun to the exclusion of working for my degree was now being questioned. I was now getting some serious grief from the Department of Economics, that I hadn't handed in any work for almost a year and they required a whole bunch of essays and such like before they would let me into my final year. The days of bullshitting my way out of corners was over.

How, I don't know, but I did have a skill in Economics, and was able to knock off these essays, but I knew I was in last chance saloon.

I was walking home from the union one night, under the bridge, Senghenydd Rd, into Glynrhonnda St. As I walked in the door it just felt that the sheen had been taken off, the lounge, and my bedroom were , well just rooms now, days of Lily , Walt, Teo, alcoholic jellies , spur of the moment parties, Adrian, the piano now all seemed a distant memory. Karma works both ways, I had pushed things to the limit, yes and now I had to pay for it. Many of my housemates were now with their heads down working, especially the scientists, and our nights out as a group were getting less and less as finals approached.

For my parents' sake, I put a huge amount of effort in during that period, even being recognised in the college and the library to a point where I did end up with a good degree. Did I deserve it? No. Did I enjoy this period in Cardiff? Oh Yes.

At this point , if I am going to write a book about my life and experiences, I really have to include this section however difficult it is to write, as I have never tried to put it in a written format before. As I said I was brought up in a very loving household and wanted for nothing. When my dad finally retired he had his police pension, and although he was not a rich man, they had holidays and a good social life etc. When he was in the Police Force dad was hugely respected in the Valley community where he settled after retirement. He involved himself in Masons, Rotary, local rugby etc and was not short of friends. I so much wanted to be like him. My mother was a different person, a very kind and caring mother and person, but for her the cup was always half empty not full, she suffered from this inferiority complex which lived with her until she died.

How does this relate to me? I have early vague recollections of sometimes just staying in my room, even at maybe 12 years of age, staring at a wall and sometimes crying for no good reason and then waking up and feeling OK again. I rationalised it by saying it was just part of growing up. I would say I wasn't feeling well , invent a cough or sore throat just to get a day off school.

When I went to college I was fine, looking forward to it and getting up to the things I have outlined in this book. I noticed there were times I used to have these palpitations and I thought I was having a heart attack combined with the fact that I was having trouble catching my breath and panicking because of that. This stayed with me for most of my early adult life. The doctors would tell me there were absolutely no physical problems with me and it was, as they said 'in my head' with no real explanation of what that meant or what to do about it. Thankfully there is more of an openess and understanding of mental health issues today, but in the 70's it was not, your average GP dealt with colds, flu's and minor ailments but you felt this was out of their league.

It did not surface all the time. These attacks defied logic I could go on a stage and sing and play with no nerves, give a talk to maybe a few hundred people with no notes and again no nerves, and like my dad , I was liked and respected and generally seen as a good guy. But underneath I was full of insecurities and self doubt. I would wake up some mornings and would just want to stay in bed or not leave my room and this might go on for days.

I am not for one minute blaming my mother for this. It may have been hereditary and something passed down in my genes. I don't want to spend a great deal of time bearing my soul, but this issue has been with me permanently and is likely to stay so. Knowing it is permanently with you, in fact helps, I therefore have to develop strategies to get me through the difficult times which thankfully are less now. However insecurities are still there at times, for example the writing of this book. I had spent a long time putting the ideas and draft together, first started writing it 4 years ago, and would be pleased with the whole concept and be excited. Then sometimes even the next minute, I would say it was no good and don't bother, you are not a writer and you are kidding yourself if you think you are... I am fortunate that a number of people have come to me for help and support in their difficult moments, perhaps because I understand what they are going through. My problem, as I guess it is with many, is that I would bottle issues up rather than get them out. The days , especially for men , of ' big boys don't cry', hopefully are things of the past and there is a greater understanding and acceptance in society now, and hopefully ,in the future.

I was worried that my teaching career was coming to a natural end. I have been in education in some format or another for nearly 40 years and what was I going to do in the future? Ok I'm approaching 70, but generally pretty healthy, don't drink or smoke, eat reasonably healthily and exercise, and hope there is some life in me yet! If you go back to the very first line of this book, I did pose the question , is this some sort of therapy? After writing this book, I probably would say it has helped me greatly. I wanted the book to be entertaining and enjoyable first, but in writing stories from

129

your past, I found it incredibly cathartic. Good or bad, I am immensely proud of writing this book. My dear wife Suzy, says it is like living with a different person and all I want to do is carry on writing, even if is for me only, but hopefully I can share my stories with others to enjoy.

If this rings a bell to anyone reading this, there is support available. But just talk to friends and family, or people who love you, it does help. You are not alone in this, there are many others who have been down this road with you, don't bottle it all up as I initially did. I became anxious when the tight lockdown started but I kept busy, teaching online and outlining this book, would I catch Covid etc came to mind, but I survived. Yes like many, there were some difficult times, but with the understanding of my wife and some close friends, I came out relatively unscathed and with a new, exciting focus in my life.

Back to Cardiff, the people I met at that time, moulded me in to the person who I was to become. I was now able to look at what kind of person I had turned out as. I was a kind and caring person, always aware of others, as some of my tales will testify. Me and Cardiff stayed in love with each other but now our relationship was different, we knew how each of us ticked. There were times that I still went back to those heady early days, but things like family and commitments were coming on the scene and changed the backcloth. But there were still jolly japes to be had, and experiences I would participate in with gusto.

There are the stories of rugby trips, especially Murrayfield, cricket with Cardiff High School Old boys, my epic cricket tours to Holland , all which are to follow. After university, I stayed in Cardiff for about another 7/8 years, but this part of my journey will end here. As new avenues opened, stories unfolded, which I will share with you in the future. My philosophy now is, 'I learn something new every day of my life', and will continue to do so.

CHAPTER 16

CARDIFF AND HOLLAND CRICKET

In the late 70's and early 80's I went on some of the most truly epic trips of my life. A bit of background. I was a reasonably competent cricketer and in 1978/9 I joined Cardiff High School Old Boys Cricket Club, for reasons I can't recall I was made club captain for that season. The Club had been in the doldrums for a while and I was charged with trying to get the club to improve, we had 2 sides and I found that the club had some good players but lacked in confidence. All I recall was looking them in the eye before the season started at a club meeting and saying that at the end of the season we would, not could, be Champions and so would our second team and we would be overall Champions of our division. There was stunned silence, I looked each in the eye and said to each individual were they with me or not ,if not I would walk through the door and move on. They all said yes and then over the season it became one of the proudest times of my sporting career. Sometimes in life you do not realize the skills you have and there are plenty of people to put you down but stick to your beliefs.

I had, and perhaps still do suffer from this lack of confidence, hence this book being 30 years in the making. Whether you enjoy it, which I hope you do, I am just proud to have eventually done it.

1979 wasn't the easiest year for me, my first child was due later in that year, and work was pressurised as I had this drive to get to the top, but I still took the captaincy on.

League cricket on a Saturday was quite demanding and during the week it took a great deal of time, training, practice, selection meetings etc. I knew that I still had this element of mischief lurking below the surface . A few blokes I knew played for a' friendly' social club on a Sunday, no home, played all their games away and were made up of guys who had the same philosophy as me. A team called the Druids, and there my friends a whole new world opened up for me. The Druids used to tour every May Bank Holiday for a week, firstly in the UK and then some bright spark said they play cricket in Holland and we should go there. The team was made up of an eclectic group of blokes including solicitors, professional guys, to students, manual workers , shop workers, etc but we were just Druids and that bond kept us together always.

There is an adage in sport ' What goes on in tour stays on tour'. This principle applies here but despite that there are stories to tell, not surprisingly most of these involved me .All our tours (we eventually did 4) tended to start in Cardiff with a pre tour club dinner, in various places in town. It involved speeches , copious amounts of red wine, and general mayhem. I lived in Cardiff for the first few tours. In those days we went by coach and ferry, it was a bloody long trip. It usually started from Cardiff in the early hours, to get to whichever ferry port was best at the time. Newhaven to Dieppe was a particularly hard run. This whole trip took about 18 hours just to get there. We were always based in the lovely Dutch city of Utrecht.

The first problem was we had been drinking most of the night and we needed a pee stop about 6 times before we left Cardiff, plus every service station we could make, plus general stops along which ever motorway we were using. The driver became an integral part of this trip, for the first 3 tours we had the same guy called Tony.

After a long and tedious bus trip our tour always started as soon as we got on the Ferry, maybe about 15/20 of us. Always a good combination of singers and artists attached, what more do you need apart from endless bars, open all the time and a bunch of blokes who just wanted to play…One memorable trip we started singing in the main packed bar, there was even a live band on board, I cheekily asked if I could borrow the mic, a musician myself, I promised to look after it, as all musicians, are rightly , possessive about their equipment. The guy understood and he was a good lad, by the end of the trip he was as pissed as us and let me borrow his guitar, out rolled the old favourites, American Pie, Sweet Caroline and karaoke type singalongs. I was now in my element, getting all and sundry up to sing. One lady came up, no idea what her name was, a solid lady from Merthyr and whispered to me she had never sang in front of anybody before, a few early morning vodkas had given her the courage and she whispered in my ear that she would love to sing 'Unchained Melody'. All her family were there and instinct told me this was a big deal to her. The 3 piece band which by now I was in charge of all came back on stage to back her . I knew the song on guitar as did the drummer and the other guitarist. She was shaking when I gave her the mic took a deep breath. We played quietly in the background so she could be centre stage, and she sang one of the best versions of the song I had ever heard, she grew in confidence . I could see her family in front almost with their jaws on the floor. I presume hubby , who was also a big lad, and had obviously frequented a few Merthyr pubs in his day, was beaming with pride and affection.

She finished, the whole bar was quiet for a few seconds, then everyone on their feet were clapping and cheering and years later, when I thought about this, I realised what a big deal this was for this lady. Centre stage , letting it rip her family so proud. It was one of those magic moments . I didn't want to come across in this book as a me me egotist but someone who got his enjoyment from giving others a chance. She asked if she could go on an she was in full flow now and knocked out I think 'I Believe', problem was the vodkas were beginning to take hold and it was getting a bit of a drunken ramble. I got her to stop then so she didn't lose the memory of the first song, she sat down flushed, happy and proud and I hope her holiday followed the same pattern.

133

I recall the end of this trip as we were coming into Dieppe, getting almost the whole boat on a conga, going well, until the captain was not too pleased when I wanted to Conga around the Captains deck as we were docking.

The bus journey through France and then Holland was easily forgettable, a lot of the younger guys had never left Cardiff or Caerphilly before and they were highly excited. Holland is not Wales, it is the flattest bit of land I have ever seen, and as we were travelling it gave me an idea for the tour t shirt....

There are so many stories to tell on 4 trips I could write a book on the tours alone, so I will try and regail a few of the more publishable ones to give you a flavour!!

On the first tour we must have arrived late at night, tired, thirsty and hungry. The manager was a small guy who looked at about 20 or so, fairly large Welshmen and wondered what the hell he had let loose in his little hotel...

This was not a bunch of hooligans who was going to trash his hotel as he quickly found out, in fact he became an integral part of the tour and loved it all. Suffice to say he had never seen anything like us before, it was too late for the kitchen to cook so he offered to made some sandwiches at least, he asked how many we wanted and we asked for about at least a metre high of them, he laughed, we were serious so he and his wife went away and made a toppling tower of sandwiches, 20 hungry Welshmen demolished that in about 10 minutes and we sent him out for the same again. We did that 3 times.

He only had one keg in the hotel .That lasted about an hour, and we did say it was best to have at least 3 kegs on hand, plus he had some , what we found out to be dangerous, Belgian bottled beers, especially some little stumpy bottles called Duvel, which turned out to be one of the strongest lagers in the world.

We had paid a deposit for the rooms up front, some of the guys had been saving for years for this, and that night we made sure we paid the balance on all the rooms and a whip round for the mountain of stuff we had eaten and drunk at least to put his mind at rest that we were not going to cause him any problems. He realized then that he had made more money in one night than he normally makes in a month. We were his friends for a week.

The following morning we had a help yourself 'continental breakfast' some of the younger guys saw breakfast as an artery clogging fry up, lashings of toast and butter and a mug of tea.

When they realized they had to eat ham and cheese cold, bread with no butter, and bloody olives, they looked in puzzlement . He had no idea what an English Breakfast was.

To cut a long story short, one of our guys was a chef, so 3 days during the week we gave the owner a shopping list and then we cooked a full English in his kitchen. It turned out that other visitors who were there, German and Dutch mainly, wanted some of that themselves, so we cooked for all and his restaurant was busier on those mornings we cooked.

This I think now was a generation issue, we respected the fact that he had other visitors so most of our jolly japes were in town and not the hotel and some of the other residents we got to know got sucked up in our, noisy, chaotic, drunken world BUT the overriding philosophy of us all was that other people should enjoy us as well.

Anyway into town we went, my idea for the tour t shirt was that I was going to have a pile of T- shirts made saying we were on tour as the' Dutch Mountain Rescue Team' Now all of you with basic geography will know that there is not even a minor hill in Holland, certainly not anything approaching a mountain.

I got to know and love the Dutch over the years, they were a charming and as hospitable a group of people you could wish to meet. But they didn't do irony. On more than one occasion I got stopped in the street to be told that ' There are no mountains in Holland so what is your shirt about'. If you have to explain that sort of humour you have no chance....

Into town we strolled , there was a street we came to called Hardbalenstratt, to cut a long story short it was the street with big glass windows with the girls of the street selling their wares in the window. Now for young lads whose limit of entertainment was Caerphilly High Street on a wet Saturday night and the only place with big windows was Caerphilly Working Men's Club, this was Never Never Land for them. Now I was not particularly well travelled but I had given a talk on Economic Development to Utrecht University some years previously and had an idea what these places were about. I don't want to sound Mr Goody Two Shoes but I had never availed myself of these services then or after...

For those of you who know Utrecht it is a wonderful city of canals which cut through the city with regular typical tiny bridges to get from one side of the canal to another. The sides of the canal is a myriad of bars, cafes and restaurants. We headed down some steps and just chose the nearest that could accommodate 20 thirsty Welshmen. Lager by the bucket prevailed followed by the most evil combination which was a bottle of Duvel, which was about 10% alcohol and you had to chase it down with a Dutch spirit called Jenever, like a Dutch Gin . The combination was rocket fuel, plus endless lagers. Anyway as you do we decided to sing, now we had come prepared with songsheets , some Welsh, there were no catchy Dutch songs we found. Amongst us there were a whole pile of good singers, a number of us sang in Male Voice choirs as well so we started singing, now this was an unusual experience for the cool café crowd in the City, but we sang well and in good harmonies and people stopped and listened, at the end of songs people were clapping and asking for more..

Above us, people were stopped above the bar and I remember a clinking sound and people were starting to throw coins at the end of each song!!. Now I grabbed a mug and started to put this money in there, this was the days of Dutch Guilders. That encouraged us even more and the next thing we knew people were pulling up chairs and joining in. Now the Dutch are pretty good at languages, especially English but when we gave them the words of Calon Lan and Myfanwy, that floored them, the night went on and on and on, the bar were more than happy and then drinks just appeared, eventually we decided to find the yellow brick road home, I was still hanging on to the mug for grim death which was now nearly full, some notes as well, like many cities there were beggars everywhere, I went off on my own and I remember coming to one guy, he broke my heart, he only had one leg and the other was deformed and he had a few cents in an old tin. Now you feel sorry for all people who have ended up this way ,but you can't help everybody so I sat with him for a while, not a brilliant experience ,then a few others joined. I then put some money in the centre of them , it was obvious that they had never seen so much money. I asked a Dutch guy who was with us to explain that they had to share it equally .

I then took the rest of the money and went into a nearby supermarket and bought as much food as I could, lots of water but no booze. It was an enormous amount of stuff, I went back and put that in the middle of the group which had now grown bigger and the Dutch guy explained again it was for them all to share.

I then left to go back to the hotel and felt again that I had done the right thing, we hadn't cured the world' s problems but we had at least helped a few people have a better day.

I got back to the hotel and none of the guys asked where the money was, because all of us would have done the same thing. I slept well.

Back at CHSOB, we DID win both the first and second team championships and won the overall team of the year, to my recollection for the first time ever. At this time I had moved to Bristol to work, as my mother would say 'Up England Way' but came back for the presentation of the awards. I was highly delighted as you can imagine, sometimes it is not a question of ability but confidence, I have applied those same principles to my teaching .If you think you are not good enough then you act like it, it just becomes a self fulfilling prophesy, break that cycle and you are half way there..

I am going to make this 2 chapters, so read on for our visit to Amsterdam and The Druids epic breakfast to finish this tour.

CHAPTER 17

MORE IN HOLLAND ..

Continuing the visit to Holland, we did actually play cricket on these trips. In this particular year we played about 4 games in the week. The Dutch are actually quite good. Hockey being the main game , and guys who played had little finesse but excellent hand eye co-ordination which meant when they hit it , the ball went a bloody long way.

One team presented us with a man of the match award. Our Captain one year, Richard won it, where else in the world would you get a prize of a jar of pickled herrings and a box of 120 black condoms?, Great present for the wife I thought… Anyway some we won, some we lost but jolly japes were had by all.

But I want to take you, dear reader, to our day off where we decided to take a train to Amsterdam for the day. Remember some of the lads had barely left Caerphilly before and were naïve on the ways of the world. Out of Amsterdam station , straight walk towards Dam Square then left to the Red Light District, we got there in the day , but as soon as night came it was a different place. Funny seeing hundreds of Japanese tourists clicking their cameras at every sex shop, club, dodgy bar and coffee shop. That must have been interesting showing them to the family in Tokyo….

In the day it just looked a grubby, dirty, run down area, reminded me of Caroline Street in Cardiff, but at night it put its glad rags on and strutted its stuff…

Before we even got to Dam Square , one of the young lads said he had to buy his girlfriend a present to take home. Without us knowing he turned into the first sex shop he came to. Now to say there was not a plethora of sex shops in Caerphilly High St is an understatement.

These shops were not a gentle Ann Summers type establishment, you wouldn't bring some of this stuff out on the classic Ann Summers parties, ladies remember them? A pile of drunken married women from the valleys wondering what you do with some sort of mechanical toy? Can you imagine Dai coming back with a bellyful of beer after a session in the Working Men's Club and all he wants is a pee, fart and go to sleep to snore for Wales, and Gladys appears with this battery operated item, and trying to excite Dai with her brand new M & S winceyette nightie, whilst alluringly slipping her Primark slippers off and she passes said item to Dai who looks at it, decides to take the batteries out for his torch as it is starting to run low, turns on his side, farts again and goes off to sleep . Perhaps I'm being unfair but it is a good story anyway!!

Back to Amsterdam. If you went through the back of these shops to the ' special' area there was stuff even in your wildest dreams(or nightmares) you would not think off. I had this image of him buying one of these ' items' for his girl in the Valleys. I would have loved to be there as she opened it….end of relationship. He came out with a look on his face I find difficult to describe. He was pale and speechless, as I think his (would have been his soon to be ex) girlfriend would have been also . Luckily he bought nothing so on we went and told him to stick close to us all.

It was really busy in the narrow streets and as you guessed he and his mate, who shall remain nameless were not there. Some of the guys wanted to go to the movies, Mary Poppins it was not, well not any version of Mary Poppins that Julie Andrews was in. I lost them again and decided to retrace my steps backwards looking for them, stuck my head around various bars, nothing, then bingo about the fourth hit I found them. To say it was a gay bar was an understatement. There was more leather in there than was on the back of a herd of cows. In the middle, sat at the bar in his bloody bobble hat was , let's just call him Dave and his mate, say Pete.

They were both giggling like kids, and they told me they both needed a pee and had called in and asked if they could use the loo, they were very happy to let them…. As they were about to go one guy had offered to buy them a drink and they had agreed.

Now this to me was where it stopped being funny, it was fairly obvious from their eyes that something had been put in their drinks and they were surrounded by guys with their arms around them, and in the corner was a sort of dance floor with guys just groping and whatever. Now I was on my own but I had to tough it out. I grabbed them both and prayed there was not going to be any bother as there were some big lads there, they shouted at me but it was handbags at 10 paces, so I dragged them off their stool and pushed them out the door where we were relatively safe.

I was shaking myself and these guys were off with the fairies, and then you realised how date rape happens and you could see why. I'm no prude but the lowlife in these swamps needed to be stamped out, there were incidents that happened that caused the Dutch Police to get a bit tighter over the years.

You know you are getting older when Amsterdam means a canal trip listening to the story of Ann Frank rather down this cess pit.

But there was humour, we went for something to eat after the guys had seen Mary Poppins, great meal and the wine and Duvel was flowing. One of the guys , it was his 21st Birthday so we clubbed together to buy him a present, remember he was up for this and older than the other two lads, and we had enough to buy him some time with one of the street girls. Off we went, it was my job to negotiate with the madam, anyway suffice to say we booked him 30 minutes with one of the girls, I went to see this girl and the room was the saddest place I had ever seen, a bed, a sink , soap and kitchen roll. It looked like you were going to the doctors. I shall not say in here but I outlined what she could and couldn't do. I'll call this guy 'Mike' he was up for this, no commitments at home with wife or girlfriend and he was up for the craic of it.

Like you do I paid the madam and in he went, we were all outside and what we did was rather than just stand there we started singing, We were singing things like ' Guide me o thy Great redeemer and ' We shall overcome' and finished with the Welsh National Anthem… The funniest point was about 20 minutes in, he was in a front room on the first floor, and all we saw was his arm coming up the mirror with a massive thumbs up sign!!

He came down after 30 minutes, he did not offer the gory details but he apparently enjoyed himself and then we wended our way to catch the last train back to Utrecht …

We had decided that we were going to finish our tour, not with a club dinner, but a club breakfast, the chef amongst us was going to cook a full English, as always there were rules. Remember we were called the Druids, so the dress code was you had to dress like a Druid, which in essence was just a white sheet off the bed, you had to wear nothing underneath, all you were allowed was a belt to keep the sheet on. A couple, I think Dutch , were invited to this dinner/ breakfast. We did adapt the rules for the lady involved where she could keep her underwear on. I have to say she was up for wearing nothing like the boys, but her husband was a little concerned, and he told her she had to keep it on. If I remember it was their wedding anniversary. I bet they didn't expect to be drinking copious amounts of red wine at about 9 in the morning, dressed in a sheet. The other rule was everyone had to do a toast to whoever or whatever you wanted…

So we got up early and decided to go for a walk into town, the sight of about 20 grown men dressed in a sheet, acting as if was the natural thing to do of a morning, got some interesting looks from the normally reserved Dutch. We even called in to one of our bars for a quick beer. Can you imagine if we were in the days of smartphones..

Anyway, down we sat, let's say it was a memorable occasion. Everyone made a toast, we were down to toasting someone's budgies birthday, or toasting the fact it was Friday.The owner toasted the 'crazy Welshmen', he was smiling at the bloody profit he made that week… The Dutch lady said it was the best wedding anniversary she had ever had, a good story to tell when she got home!!! As we were going that afternoon ,we rebooked the hotel for 2 years time. As you can imagine there are many tales to tell over about 8 years, but enough is enough.

We got on the bus later that night, suffice to say it was a quiet trip home, even on the ferry we were basically knackered and no fun was to be had.

When we all got back to Cardiff or Caerphilly, when asked what kind of trip we had, we all just said ' Oh it was OK'…..'What happens on tour stays on tour'….

Then my dear readers off I went from Utrecht to a warm and balmy March day in Edinburgh for another Murrayfield trip…

CHAPTER 18

MURRAYFIELD

This tale started in early 1975. At that time I was actually in the old Glamorgan Polytechnic in Treforest , on a one year course to become a careers officer. Immediately before that ,straight from college, I was working at Eagle Star insurance in Newport Road as a graduate trainee. But I knew I was not long from packing in to start my education career. There I had met a guy Dave ,who played rugby for Old Penarthians and he asked me to go over as they needed someone for my position, I was getting a bit unhappy at Llandaff where I was playing, so over I went, I quite enjoyed it there. In a few weeks I was playing OK, scored a try and became set in the first team.

Dave then said it was Murrayfield in a few weeks and he had 2 tickets and had booked some B& B and did I want to go, only problem is that we had to take the red eye from Cardiff on Friday night, so I thought why not ,turned out to be a big mistake, but I will let the tale unfold.

We had arranged to go up on the overnight Friday train arriving in Edinburgh early Saturday morning. Dave gave me a strange request, he told me to wear or bring some smart clothes, shirt tie jacket etc,. I had no idea why but I was going to find out... We met in the afternoon of Friday at the Old Arcade, our train was early evening. I was wearing tidy clothes, which seemed overdressed for a long train ride and just took a few bits extra in a carrier bag.

I decided to get some food for the journey so off we went for a few sandwiches from Hayes Island, which were my favourite, and headed to the station. By the time I had got there I had eaten them all, so I had to call in Asteys to get a few more, the only beer we could get then was one of those party cans of 7 pints of Watney's Red Barrel, what could be better dear reader than a large tin of warm Watneys? Especially as we didn't have anything to take the top off, no ring pulls in those days.

Dave had a striking resemblance to the Welsh winger , Gerald Davies, and he said that it would get us free drinks etc on the train. He bypassed the small problem that Gerald Davies was playing for Wales the next day, and his pre match activities would probably not include the red eye to Edinburgh on a friday night...

I was wrong.... He played the law of averages, I'll explain later, I realised the problem ahead when we got to Cardiff station, it was packed , a sea of red as far as the eye could see, were we going to get on ?

I am sure some people reading this who were on this trip would back me up. Anyway we did get on, and just about managed to get a seat, well we had to share, the smell of stale beer, greasy butties and body odour was not the finest smell I had ever inhaled.

Off we went. The problem was I needed a pee and we hadn't hit the next stop yet. The loo was a place to avoid at all costs, anyway I eventually got back to the seat and lo and behold he had girls around him and he was bloody signing autographs as Gerald Davies. These girls had no idea and with a straight face he said he was in the programme , but they hadn't had time to change it due to an injury, and he was supposed to stay at home but decided at the last minute to go up, all the flights were booked, and this is all he could get, and they believed him!! I didn't know where to look...

Then they were sharing drinks with him and I was left with the warm Watney's Red Barrel which I couldn't even open, deep joy...

It was a long trip, Dave aka Gerald was as pissed as a parrot... We got off eventually and he told me , to wash and brush up before we went into the City. I was seriously worried what was coming next.

To be honest I have never seen so many people in one place, just a sea of humanity. We got to Princes Street which was a fair walk, and parallel to it was the street with the bars/ hotels, I think it was Rose St. I was still with Dave at this time, although my instinct was telling me not to. We came to one of the best hotels in town, way out of my league, called, if I recall, The Balmoral. We went in and it was chaos, this was part of his plan. He told me to stay close , from a distance he was looking at the keys hanging up at reception and logging the ones that were there as these people were obviously out . He winked at me and told me to follow him. He then pulled me to the main dining room, obviously it was busy and the waiters were under stress and he just asked for the best table they had , and he was in room whatever. If you look the part, I realised you can get away with murder. If we had turned up in Welsh shirts with beer all over them , no doubt we would not have got in but it was obvious he had done this sort of thing before.

We sat down, someone came with a menu, and the prices were more than most people earned in a month. He ordered something ridiculous and a bottle of wine which would be expensive if it was that price today. He even complained that the starters were taking too long. I was mortified, I am, and was, basically honest and this was just cheating and conning people.

I told him I was going to the loo, went to reception and said the guy on table whatever is not a resident and he is conning them out of a meal… He asked my name etc, but I was through the door and in the crowds as quick as I could.

I got up to plenty of japes, but nothing this deceptive. My dad would have been mortified if I had taken part in this, so I am glad I never got involved . I never saw him again after that weekend thankfully, as I was leaving rugby for other commitments.

Anyway I am now in the middle of Edinburgh, a little bit of money, no ticket and no idea where to go, so just follow the throng, I walked down Rose St, tried to call in the odd bar but it was impossible, it felt that Wales was empty, and they were all in that street. It turned out that this was the last

International you could pay at the gate, Wales were in their pomp, they had just come off 2 great lions tours in 71 and 74, and all the great Welsh players were playing and the whole of Wales wanted to see them.

It is one hell of a walk to the stadium, I was quite late and close to kick off, and the sight when I got there was jaw dropping. The gatemen had given up the ghost and people were just pouring in to get to see the game, I remember a grass bank you had to get up and go down the other side. All I saw were people pushing the masses up the hill to get over the top to see the game, I was not too bad in crowds then but that soon changed as there was no room to even breathe. I got as far as the top, and on tiptoe I could just about see a corner of the field.

Then I heard a loud scream and there were about 4 or 5 girls in a huddle and one of them was on the floor, I looked at her and basically she was in the middle of a panic attack, she couldn't catch her breath and for those who have had one of these (me included) I knew how distressing this can be. I went to her, she was quite small and I just lifted her on my shoulder and pushed my way back down the hill as everybody was trying to get up. In fairness many people realised there was a problem and let me past.

I got to a patch which was relatively quiet and sat her up, I knew what to do in these situations, she was awake now, and I just asked her to concentrate and slow her breathing down. I was whispering in her ear now to slow right down and breathe calmly. Some of her friends came to check but once they realised she was alright they went back to the game. We sat for about 10 minutes, the game had started, I held her hand, some colour was coming to her face, and I sensed we were over the worst, but I was still constantly telling her to breathe slower. It was beginning to work it may have been 20 minutes or so and then she got up and was hanging on to me for grim death.

Found that her name was Rosie, she lived in the City and had come with friends. We walked out of the ground and

147

thankfully the crowds had gone , found a café, got tea and a cake and just sat there until she was able to chat. She was a lovely little thing and she was worried that I had missed the game, but to be honest I wouldn't have lasted long anyway, eventually she wanted to buy me a drink, so we walked away from the ground and went to a bar.

She was incredibly grateful , I was just happy she was OK, we talked a little and I said what had happened and I wasn't sure where I was going to stay that night till I could get a train on the Sunday, at that point she went to a phone and came back and said I was staying with her.

Please don't jump to any conclusions here, she lived with her mum and dad on the outskirts of the city and in about an hour her dad was coming to pick us up at some prearranged place, by which time the match would have just about finished.

To be honest the whole day was catching up with me now and I was knackered, tired , hungry and thirsty. Her dad picked us up, said hello, he was Malcolm and within 1 minute I must have crashed out. The next thing I remember was someone shaking my shoulder as we had arrived at this lovely house in the leafy suburbs, mum was called Veronica and they had a younger son whose name I can't remember. They had prepared a room for me, asked for my clothes and I crashed out and they had my clothes washed and ironed by the time I woke up.

Went downstairs and Rosie and her Mum put their arms around me and thanked me for everything I had done, there followed a brilliant night, dinner was amazing and wine and whisky flowed freely, she was a different girl now and was very pretty, OK it was just a fleeting thought!!

Best night's sleep I had ever had. When I woke up, Malcolm called me to one side and thanked me again. This had been an issue with Rosie for some time and I just said a bit of specialist support and she would be fine, I had trained as a counsellor, and was happy to offer advice. He had paid for me to take a different train back and had put me on first class for the most comfortable journey I had ever had. I didn't help her for any reward but I have to say it was very much appreciated!!

We became good friends, she trained as a primary teacher which she loved, she married a pilot , moved abroad, went on to have 3 kids and I kept in touch with her for some time after that..

Dear reader, I'll finish by reminding you of the concept of Karma which Walt taught me, be good to others and things will be good for you. I still hold that dear to my heart.

P.S Wales lost 12-10 so I didn't miss anything anyway.....

I couldn't think of a concise name for the next chapter , so read on for Rugby, Monasteries and Bingo....

CHAPTER 19

RUGBY , MONASTERIES AND BINGO

Rugby in my College days was an integral part of my world, and strangely in many ways a lot of my Rugby trips I preferred to do on my own. I have mentioned a few times on here about my accident which I had before University. If I am writing about me and my experiences in those days, I have got to talk about that accident and the effect it had on me , however painful it may be as I have not written in detail about it before.

I was a decent schoolboy player. I followed my dad who played and was Vice Captain of Bridgend in the late 40's and was heavily involved in the development of rugby in the South Wales Police. One of my prized possessions is a book he wrote called ' A century on the Rugby Beat' which was a history of rugby in the Police forces of South Wales. His Rugby knowledge was encyclopedic. He could recall the Welsh side who played Scotland in 1935, but ask him what he had for dinner yesterday and he wouldn't have a clue, mum used to lay out his clothes for him each day, and until later life he would rarely go out without a tie on. I had played well in the Sandfields team in 69 and early 70 and with my cricket, plus I was a decent high jumper as well meant that a career in sport was mapped out.

In the Summer of 1970, Dad got me job in a local factory which was just starting in the area, fairly mindless stuff, I know the name of the company which I shan't repeat here but they made industrial size air conditioning units for steelworks and large cold storage units . I went on a few jobs away with them which were stories on their own.

I was getting bored there ,but it was just for a few months, I had enjoyed my trips out which I describe later, and I was happy I was coming towards the end in about July 1970 . To cut a long story short, a forklift truck reversed and didn't see me and ran over the top of my left foot. All I recall was screaming in pain and then passing out. My next recollection was waking up in an ambulance with a mask over me, and my dad holding my hand next to me. I felt no pain and must have been on heavy painkillers. I cannot remember the next period of time. I remember waking up in hospital looking down with my left leg in plaster on heavy traction and thankfully dad was still there. I asked him if I was OK and he said I would be fine.

A few days later I was at least awake and only then did dad tell me the full story. The injury was serious, I had 24 fractures in my foot alone and it was about 3 inches shorter than my right foot. And without my knowledge they were discussing with my Dad whether to amputate my left foot. I loved him anyway but he had said to the doctors that that was not going to happen and they had to find a way to try and save it. Other doctors were called in and the state of medical knowledge at the time meant that there was only one possibility to save my foot which was basically piece the bones together like a jigsaw and put a series of metal pins through it to hold it in one piece until the bones had healed. This operation had never been done before in the area, and it was the only chance I had, my dad immediately signed for it, and then the following day I was due for this operation which in the end took about 9 hours. My recollection was that I had been transferred to Rhydlafar hospital where these specialists were based. Obviously the next few weeks were a blur, but I remember being told that because my bones were young it was starting to knit and with careful therapy I would be able to walk again, but they had no idea whether I would have a limp or any other long term problems. I have a big lump of bone on the side of my foot which means choice of shoes is limited!! And I have no feeling in a few of my toes.

Before that accident I must tell you a story, in fact two stories. As I said the company made large air conditioning units. They had a job which was putting air conditioning units in to the monastery on Caldey Island just off Tenby. It was a monastery run by Cistercian monks, who I believe still own the island. There were only about 40 permanent residents, mostly Monks and a few farm workers on the Island. The engineer , Mike needed a gofer and that suited me. So off we went. We had to drive to Tenby which was , and presumably still is, a popular tourist resort. Now Caldey Island was about half a mile from Tenby and you had to catch a ferry to get on there, there were no cars on the island apart from a few trucks they used for gardening etc. The other major problem for us was because of the tides there were no ferries after about 6 pm, so we could see the twinkling lights of Tenby but at to stay on this Island in a bloody monastery, where the accommodation was basic to say the least. We were put at the top of this tower and apparently there was a rumour that this place was haunted, just what you needed, so there we are at the top of a tower with the wind swirling around, poor, almost non existent lighting, plus no beer. Mike smoked and he was not even allowed to have fags on him. It was destined to be a long ,long week. Monastic groups or clans or whatever you call a group of monks, I had, and still have, no idea what they were about. Basically it was a worldwide group with a head honcho who was an Abbot. (I did do some research here and they were Cistercian monks but I still had no idea what the different Monk groups were). If you had been a bad boy in another monastery, you were sent to Caldey as a sort of penance. A small island on the Welsh coast wasn't the pinnacle of Monastic life. So you had Father this, Father that, one was in charge of gardening, one in charge of cooking, one fishing and so on. We were nervous enough in this bloody tower, so you can imagine how we felt on the first morning when the chanting and prayers started at 5.00 in the morning !! Whichever Father was in charge of cooking did not go the Gordon Ramsey school of excellence. Eggs were like bullets, it may have started off as a pig but what this bacon ended up as defied description , I presumed the red slimy stuff was tomato but you never knew. At least we didn't have to sit with them to eat, so we took a plate outside, if you want to lose weight join a monastery.

It turned out they were an interesting lot. They had a tourist shop where they sold a whole pile of stuff usual tourist tat plus they did a special Caldey perfume and chocolate, made on the Island. What really happened was this stuff used to come in large jars from France I think, and all they did then was pour this liquid into smaller bottles then sell it at rip off prices in the shop. Father Entrepreneur used to run this, and this shop made a blinding profit from unsuspecting tourists who thought they had this special perfume lovingly made by the monks, when it was poured into bottles from a large jar, brilliant. Mike and I could never remember their proper names so it was Father Fish or Father Spade who did the garden or Father Wimpy who was the cook and so on.

Mike and I often worked outside. It was a big job, they were turning an old store room into a refrigerated room to store veg etc. It wasn't a cheap job, but with the rip off prices in the shop it was no surprise they could afford it !! Mike was a great guy and I really liked him. He had a typically blunt Valley humour. One little kid came up to him, poked him in the shoulder and asked him ' Oi are you a Monk mister? I don't think that F.... Off you little shit' was the response he was expecting and he ran off to tell his mum what this nasty monk said. He WAS a little shit, and his mother never came to see us, as I think Mike's response would have been no different to her.

Mike was also pretty shrewd, he was as pissed off as me about not having a drink and smoke with Tenby so close. We had each been given an allowance by the firm, so far we had spent naff all, the monastery cost us nothing and we couldn't buy fags and booze, so he decided to work really hard for few days, get ahead of the game, and stay over in Tenby for a night which we duly did. Got over early one day, found a cheap B & B, and had a great day in Tenby, a lovely town, we drank and ate great steaks, and remember 'Surf and Turf'?

We had that in a Berni Inn in Tenby. In between Mike chain smoked and took a few packs back to the Island. Great night, the following morning after a glorious nights sleep, we had full English plus lashings of doorstop bread and butter dunked in the egg. And then back to the Island with a bag full of beers and wine to keep us sane until we got home. There was one Father who saw us having a beer one evening, now alcohol was taboo, but I suppose this is why he was sent to Bad Monks Island. He had a few and told us he had been trying to make his own , like an illicit whisky, he became known as Father Poteen. Bless you father.

Anyway we got through it and I have to say, because of Mike we made the best of it…

The other trip I did with Mike was one of the scariest and funniest. It was to the steelworks in Scunthorpe, now at that time if you had given the world an enema they would have put the pipe in Scunthorpe . We stayed in a B&B which was basic to say the least, with a landlady who had somewhere along the line lost her social skills with customers. The list of what you couldn't do was endless, in by such a time, no 'visitors', no noise after 11, breakfast between 8 and 8.30 or forget it etc. Anyway where do you go on a wet Wednesday night in downtown Scunthorpe? The only place was the local Working men's club, it was easier to get into Fort Knox. Mike explained that we were up for a few days working in the steelworks, he had to show proof that we were and I had to prove I was over 18, which I was only just, and after half an hour we were allowed temporary membership.

It was one of the biggest places I had ever seen, like an aircraft hanger and just lines and lines of tables. Service was at the table which I had never seen before and I suppose the nearest thing I can compare it to was the Wheeltappers and Shunters Social Club which was on TV a few years later. It was packed and it was bingo hour, now those of you who play and have played Bingo will know how seriously people take it. With the amount of people there the prizes were enormous and certainly worth winning. Mike and I decided not to play with the thought that if an outsider won, we would not get out alive. I watched the whole thing with complete fascination. When it started you could hear a pin drop. They all had these 'daubers'(or dabbers) which was an essential bingo tool. You are talking maybe 400 people playing, when you had a line the prize was about 100 pounds, so stakes were high. The acoustics were brilliant as no one wanted to miss anything. There were an amazing number of people involved in this and I genuinely was amazed at the skill you needed to be a bingo caller, not too slow not too quick, be clear, add all the jargon like legs 11 , 2 fat ladies 88, 21 key of the door etc, every number seemed to have a code of some sort. The caller was brilliant at raising the tension as the numbers were called, you almost sensed when a line was nearly completed and when someone shouted 'house' you could hear general hubbub and looking where this person was sitting. I was living and breathing it with them and I wasn't even playing!! I remember when it was for a full house and the prize was maybe 300 pounds or so, a King's ransom to anybody at that time. The silence was electric, I was transfixed, no one, but no one ,looking anywhere but at their card, no conversation but totally fixed only on the caller and your numbers. Years later when I was studying and teaching Psychology and when we were discussing addiction, I often used that time as an example. As each number was called the atmosphere was more and more tense, then someone shouted 'house' and the whole place would be looking at where the call was from, the tension had still not finished as the assistant was checking each number with the caller but when the call was deemed correct the person who won was beaming as this wasn't a few quid. It was serious money. Then the next thing that happened also amazed me, that card was ripped off and the whole cycle would start again.

Going back to how it was dangerous. The main job we had was fixing the air conditioning units in the many cranes used in the steelworks. We couldn't wait for the cranes to stop working , they carried massive steel ingots and rolls around the plant . It was hot and dangerous work and the air con in the cab had to be working. So we had to climb up this crane and work as best we could in the cab with the crane operator. Now I was not too good with heights, but I had to learn pretty quick as I had to pass Mike various tools. Health and Safety would have a fit now. Mike sometimes had to get out of the cab and fix things from the outside. I dare not look down and I couldn't let Mike down, he had done it for years and was obviously good at what he did. I had to learn quickly to depend on others and I suppose that was a trait that I had to develop through my life. When people said to me they or their Dad worked in the steel works at least I had a small glimpse of how dangerous this work was and the respect these people deserved. When I had a class of maybe difficult kids I then used to consider these guys and miners ,and realise I had no idea what danger others had to face on a daily basis and I had nothing to moan about…

Not long after I came back from the second of 2 Scunthorpe trips with Mike my accident happened…

…. But in every situation I tried to look at the humour. I at least managed to get to Uni on time in the October of 1970. With this still heavy plaster , but two feet at least. I was involved in the fun and frolics albeit slowly. Now the CRI was not my hospital and they didn't have my notes, so when I broke the plaster all they would do would wrap another bit of plaster round it until I had my regular checks in Rhydlafar . It just got bigger and bigger and I had to drag the bloody thing around. I knew I had the pins in my foot but somehow I thought they would dissolve. Little did I know that as the bone was healing it was pushing this pin out, so I would look down and there was this bloody metal pin coming through my shoes. !! I thought jees we can rebuild him.. I had to go to the CRI and eventually they would pull these pins out with pliers (stop thinking about it, it was me with the bloody pins!!). Anyway no one told me there were 8 of these damn things in there, so I would see the same nurse each time, she would smile and pull the next one out. I kept these pins in a little tin and when the last one came out Nurse Gladys Emmanuel or whatever she was called ,was as pleased as I was. Never one to miss an opportunity I asked her did she want to go out for a drink to celebrate, she said she had a boyfriend, but that had never stopped me in the past, and we did have some jolly japes together for a short while. She came into my Bermuda Triangle one night and realized it wasn't for her, and eventually went back to her boyfriend. Just as well.

About 3 years later I was back on a rugby field, OK I was never going to be good enough for serious level sport but through bloody hard work, determination and never ever giving up, I still played a decent level of 2nd tier sport. Can you imagine where I would have been without my dad, living on one leg at 18, I don't even want to go down there. I'll owe him till my dying day but no more than I did during that July in 1970.

That was hard to write, but I learnt to become a survivor and as you have read I still had a life at college and beyond which I enjoyed to the full, another of those crucial 'what if' moments which define your life..

A few years later around 1972 I got back to college early that year, thankfully my leg was healing well and I was running and starting to train again but was nowhere near fit. I was in the Union bar which was not a major surprise, and the captain of the rugby team came over in a real panic. The university had to play in the first proper round of the Welsh cup competition. Most of the regular first team players had not returned to university, hence the flap. I was asked would I turn out, and with the bravado of buckets of SA, I said sure. I had no boots or kit and had been nowhere near a Rugby field for a few years due to my accident. I was not particularly worried as I assumed we were playing another fairly lowly ranked team, OK we were likely to lose but no harm done, I think both Walt and Teo were around at this time and Teo going 'I'll play, I'll play what is this rugby you talk about'? Even I was not that evil and said it was not a good idea, Walt looked fit, had never played before, so he was dragged in as a winger where he could do least damage, but he was not going to take his turban off...

To cut a long story short the team we had to play was Glamorgan Wanderers who in those days were a fairly useful first class side, this put a new dimension on the day, and we were due to play them at their ground in Ely the following Saturday. There were only about 7 of the proper Rugby team there , the rest were made up of waifs and strays like me.

We turned up , a rag tag bunch of drunkards. They looked like well, first class rugby players. I was now seriously worried as we heard them shouting in the changing room before the game. Walt was, well as pale as he could be and out we strolled. There was a large crowd there as well. You knew this wasn't going to end well. At kick off I'm trying to explain to Walt you had to pass backwards. Anyway we kicked off, luckily one of our side was a kicker and from the first lineout , somehow we won a penalty, Our kicker took it, great kick and we were 3-0 up, was a shock on the cards? Were these plucky students going to provide an upset? No. In a thankfully shortened game we lost 98-3.

Yes, that was our sole score, but we consoled ourselves later by saying at least we were in the lead, as you would expect it was men against boys, Walt lasted about 4 minutes when somehow the ball came to him, he amazingly caught it, looked up and there were about 3 no neck 18 stone Neanderthals bearing down on him. He was quick, as he saw them coming , he screamed, threw the ball to them and ran off the pitch, turban flowing to the far flung depths of the ground and there he stayed until I found him during the evening.

As you can imagine it was a complete rout and we spent the whole game behind our posts waiting for the conversion. The second half was mercifully shorter and the ref blew up about 10 minutes early. Despite it all, the whole team stuck at it and didn't just lie down and give up . I thought I was going to die. But Welsh rugby being as it was, I thought they would take the piss out of us, but they didn't , they clapped us off as if we were a top side. What we had earned was respect. We could have forfeited the game or not turned up but we didn't and for that they treated us as equals.

There followed an epic night . The food was top notch, jugs and jugs of beer were put on the table , I disappeared to fetch Walt, who was worried, he needn't have been . They put him in the middle of their group and again you wish you had a camera, 2 big guys and Walt all in his turban was a sight to behold.

We may have lost the game by over 90 points but with the drinking and singing we more than held our own. Rugby in Wales was a classless game, they were all local lads working during the last days of East Moors or the like and we were students but there was none of that you are better than us crap. They presented us with a club shirt at the end of the night and in fact I used to wander up there now and again to watch a game and always had a right royal welcome. If you remember Rita, it was one of these guys who came along to fix her plumbing for nothing. They even gave me a season ticket and I gave them tickets for some Rag week events and we became close in Rugby terms and just as blokes.

International day for me had a set routine. My dad had a good friend who was a member of the WRU and tickets were not a problem. Perhaps unconsciously I was remembering those early days which I have spoken about with dad in the early 60's. I would start in the Union but would want to get to the Old Arcade as soon as it opened. The pub was cleared of all tables and chairs and you squeezed together like sardines, social distancing it was not. But there were protocols, when you got to the front you probably had to get about 10 pints and they were passed back on some sort of invisible Brains covered magic carpet. Rarely was a drop spilled. I loved it there , the singing the good natured banter, even with the opposition supporters was awesome. If you wanted a pee it was best to judge it a least 15 minutes before you needed it as it would take that long to get there. Whoever cleaned the loo's in the morning deserved triple pay.

Leave about 15 minutes before kick off, grab a quick pie in the market then you could see the ground, clicking through the turnstiles, hearing the crowd and the band, and then you are busting for a pee and join the queue in those long metal troughs with about 100 blokes crammed into no distance. I would normally be standing in the East Terrace and then pushing your way in, to try and see, luckily I was tall and I tended to stay at the back as no doubt I would need a pee (and a pie) before half time.

First game I saw in 1970, was Scotland , the Scots were a great craic in town and added to the days considerably. On that particular day Wales had won 18-9 and it was just the beginning of those magical years where it was great to be at the games in the 70's. Wales lost the championship that year by having a poor game in Ireland, letting France win the title on points difference. The only redeeming feature that year was that England were bottom and got well and truly stuffed by Wales in Twickenham.!!

Another reason I always stood at the back was I could be first out. In this case Wales were winning comfortably, so I would go out 5 minutes early and my first port of call was the Horse and Groom in Womanby Street, nose against the door waiting for it to open. Sometimes first in, straight to the bar, would order 4 pints, all for me, then disappear to the back and that was me done. Occasionally I met people I knew but I had my own routine and was happy on my own. As everybody tended to mill around the town bars, I didn't. It was now about early evening, I would be off down my yellow brick road to the Bute and for some reason and I don't know why, I felt at home there, the pubs were quieter, probably the Marshioness of Bute or Mount Stuart which were my regular haunts. I would sit quietly there for a while, mind my own business and I always felt this inner contentment which I cannot explain to this day.

1971 was a different year, Wales took all before them then winning the Grand Slam, tight game in Scotland where John Taylor kicked that last minute conversion from the touchline. First game in Cardiff was England ,only a short time previously I had said goodbye to Lily, and she was still at the forefront of my thoughts, how I would have loved to take her there, she would have loved it and I looked around during the game expecting her to be hanging on to my arm, shouting for Wales as she had become an honorary Welsh woman, but she wasn't and a shrug of my shoulders and I recall it was the first, and only , time I just went straight home after an International....

The next tale was about my lifelong struggle with my weight, read on...

CHAPTER 20

CARRY THAT WEIGHT....

Another theme throughout my life is that I have always had issues with my weight. I didn't originally. I was thin up until I went to Uni in 1970. It would be a lie if I didn't say that the endless beer , largely junk food and snacking on crisps, pies, fried food and the like had nothing to do with it. Trousers that I got into easily, I now had to lie on the bed , take a deep breath and just about do the button up, the bottom button on your shirt stretched a bit and you knew there was no one to blame but yourself. It did pee me off that friends who were largely built like stick insects could follow the same lifestyle as me and not put on an ounce of weight.

The diet industry , especially in the 70's and 80's was a money making machine, raking in millions on the back of people's insecurities. In a sense it was a replacement for the insecurities I had about being a policeman's son, will people like me even if I am overweight.

Over those years I must have tried every fad diet in existence of which there were many, The Cambridge diet which replaced food with a drink I stuck for a few weeks, then the high or low protein diet, high carb and low fat diet and any combination you could think of. They would often work for a short time and then back to square one. I did have willpower and when I put my mind to do it ,it would work. It was all my own fault but when I would have my rare trip home mum would say you have put on some weight and tell me I had to cut down, and now I was only allowed one bowl rather than 2 of bread and butter pudding.

The funniest story here is, I can't remember exactly when and where I was but I had put on an exceptional amount of weight and decided for the first, and only ,time in my life to go to a diet club. It was Weightwatchers or something similar. There were these green foods and red foods and you were allowed certain amounts of each every day. I realized even then it was crap and it was about sensible eating.

Along I went to my first meeting, maybe about 20 women and I was the only bloke, which triggered my natural sense of devilment. The class was run by someone called ' Debbie' or the like and had been through her own problems , i.e she was now slightly less fat than she was before. The first week I sat on my own and watched , it was bloody hilarious. They went round each person who had to stand on a scales and then 'Debbie' would announce to the class that ' Phyllis' had lost half an ounce in the week, and everyone clapped so loud that you would swear she had found a cure for cancer. Then up would come ' Doreen' and Doreen had put on a pound, great rounds of ohh, ahhs, Doreen with a quivering bottom lip and me still clapping. Then it was excuse time like ' well I followed the plan to the letter but it was my budgies birthday and I celebrated with an extra chocolate digestive' , sage nodding of understanding from the rest as if they had faced the same life threatening traumas, me thinking Doreen has probably ripped through a whole packet and a few Kit Kats thrown in. I was loving this and my motivation was coming to the fore, how could I really piss these women off? The answer came when I found out that the ' slimmer of the week' is the person who lost the most weight in a week got a special gold sticker in their book towards a special half stone certificate. It was exactly like infants school where the little kids would get a sticker for ' the most helpful student of the week' fine when you are 4 but slightly different when you were 25 years or more.

Before I came to this club I had the motivation to do something about it and it was going to be my only visit , but this sticker quest gave me all the extra motivation I needed.

I went up to weigh like everybody else and there was a round of sympathetic clapping, yes I was a large lump but there were bigger lumps than me there. Anyway suffice to say my own plan of action, sensible eating, no picking and some exercise , I started to put into place.

The following week I went up to weigh and had lost about 4 pounds, I knew it was mostly fluids. The girls clapping like I was the new messiah and my gold sticker stuck firmly in my book. If it was a green shield stamp book it was the first step to new hair dryer...

Suffice to say dear reader, I won the gold sticker for 14 consecutive weeks by which time I was sitting on my own, totally ignored and not even a minor clap when I went up for my endless stickers and what turned out to be my 3 stone certificate.

I had had enough fun by now and it was time to leave, but the best was yet to happen. I got pulled aside by Debbie who said it was best I left as I was demoting the rest as they never had a chance of winning the sticker and many of them had put on weight. So I said, hang on so it is now MY fault that these women had put on weight, she looked uncomfortable, but I wasn't giving up. I took out my sticker book, ripped it up and threw it in her lap, I never said much at these meetings but as I left I looked at them all and said something like 'you will always be fat until you realise it is your fault and not someone else's and until you accept that you will never win'. I then left to complete silence and never went back again.

There is a postscript, one lady who again I had never spoken to somehow got hold of me, she wrote me a letter saying she agreed with what I said and her problem was she had 3 kids in quick succession and had put on weight and couldn't get rid of it. I am not a qualified dietician , although I knew a lot about foods, and just suggested she saw a dietician , I did and she used the same one as me, I met her a few times, and she looked OK had started an exercise class and was doing special exercises to help her tum and like many young mums she tended to pick her kids food when she was feeding them. Whether she lost weight or not was not the issue but she felt happier in her own body and a bloody sticker in a book wasn't the answer.

I would like to say that I never had any problems after that but I continued to yo yo with my weight. The major time for me was when someone said to me, a diet is not the answer, diets by their nature have a beginning and an end, I had to change lifestyle. I don't drink, don't smoke, do exercise, don't even like fried food or chocolate and it still fluctuates , but so be it. It has never affected my relationships over the years, people you care about look to the person, and not the size you are, and I feel comfortable now in my own body.

This is not a how to lose weight chapter . The west is still obsessed by weight and the model industry and media has a lot to answer for by equating thin with success, money, fame etc. There is still a worrying trend in anorexia amongst boys as well as girls and the media have a lot to for answer for.

The only advice as someone who has been though it is:

'Don't Kid Yourself', do not equate size with being a good person as that is what people will remember you by.

I will finish with just a tour of random memories of my growing up period , hope they ring some bells with you..

CHAPTER 21

MY FINAL THOUGHTS OF
GROWING UP IN WALES IN
THE 50'S ,60'S AND 70's

In this last chapter I am attempting to put how I saw the 50's to the 70's from my perspective living in Wales . The early part of the 50's I don't remember, being born in 1952, but towards the end I was 8, and in the 60's I went from 9 to just before 18. The 60's were the most significant decade for me, Wales and the UK in general. The 50's still had the effects of the second world war to deal with , rationing carried on till 1954, and diets were limited to what mum could do with limited ingredients. Bland is the best description, spices were unheard of and perhaps they came to Cardiff quicker than the rest ,as the immigration from the West Indies, Africa, India and Ceylon in those days brought a cornucopia of spices and smells which were to change British eating habits forever. It never really got to my mother though as she felt this spicy food was 'The food of the Devil'. That generation would seem racist now, but they knew no different , especially in the Valleys.

The 50's were a black and white decade whilst the 60's were technicolour. In the 60's it was the first generation of young people free of conscription, their parents had fought in the war to give this generation the freedom to argue, disagree, demonstrate against much that was bad in the world especially for me apartheid in South Africa, the despots of Africa such as Idi Amin. Did I appreciate that my parents generation had allowed us to do what we were doing? Again I speak for myself and would say no not at that time.. Even at my age now, I have been able to do what I did over the years because that generation allowed me and perhaps only now do I really appreciate it.

One of the biggest changes was undoubtedly music. The decade of rock and roll was again a catalyst for change, The Beatles especially in 1967 when Sgt Peppers came out and then the influence of Bob Dylan, The Beach Boys and many others plus the early Elvis. It is such a tragedy that he turned into a caricature of the rock and roll genius he was in the mid 50's with Sun Records. Even the Beatles late in the 60's were questioning the system with albums like Revolution, and Lennon asking us to 'Give Peace A Chance'

Strangely for me I went down another route and didn't get sucked into that world and was into the old Delta Blues Men of the 30's and 40's and it was them who rocked my boat, few of my friends were like that and I suppose my need to go my own way started then. Young people were starting to stand up for their beliefs and individuality. But ,and it is a big but, the Valleys of Wales was not London where Carnaby street, people like Mary Quant and Twiggy ruled the roost, but tight Valley traditions were not going to change overnight because of flower power .

However Cardiff was seeing changes, although seen by London as a bit of a backwater, Cardiff had its own vibrant scene, especially in the late 60's and 70's , shops like Chelsea Girl appeared in Cardiff and the red heart of the shop became a beacon for young girls, queuing to get in the Top Rank where their leather look white boots and skirts up to your bum were common sights. Even us trendy young men were in to flared , hipster trousers, mine mainly from C and A, girls in their crushed velvet bell bottoms, so cool .

However my first recollection of singing in public was at an Urdd Eisteddfod at either Swansea in 1964 or Aberavon in 1966. I was at Garw grammar for both. You had to sing in Welsh, and somewhere from the depths of my memory I remember the song we sang it was called ' Tresaith' which is a small village , god knows where in Wales ,and what the song was about, I have no idea, we didn't win but I had a certificate..

My other musical memory was back to Pontardawe, to my parents eternal credit (again) I wanted a guitar one Christmas and I got one , a basic acoustic but I was overjoyed, no one in our family had any musical background,(later all my 3 children had music lessons and became excellent musicians themselves) .Anyway I used to sit in my room for hours with Bert Weedon's book of chords and made some horrendous noises. Luckily the Police station where we lived was quite big so I could pluck away to my heart's content knowing that I was going to be the world's next Elvis ...

Eventually I could knock out a tune and in Pontardawe there was one of the most popular folk clubs around. You know the kind of place, some very intense people , hand over one ear singing some dirgy lament which had about 100 verses. They had open mic nights and I plucked up courage one night to play a song which had taken me about 3 months to learn. The song was 'Don't think Twice Its Alright' by Bob Dylan. I have never been so nervous in my life, but took a deep breath, closed my eyes and amazingly did a passable version which at least got a ripple of applause .

A guy who was also playing that night came over and said well done. This guy was Max Boyce. If I was really honest I didn't rate him then. He was OK but nothing special. But obviously the amazing Welsh Rugby side of the 70's was his salvation and good luck to him ,especially when 'Hymns and Arias' became his signature song. I saw him opening the 1999 World Cup at the National Stadium and I was taken back to that cramped upstairs room in Pontardawe.

I also recall a girl singing then and she had the voice of an angel and I was transfixed. A young shy girl with long blond hair. It was Mary Hopkin who went on the great things with' Those were the days'.

I practiced hard and became a reasonably good guitarist and singer, and I was writing my own stuff as well. Years later I wrote a song called ' Just One Life' which was about a particularly difficult time of my life ,and I am still proud of the song and sing it now and again.

One of those 'what if' moments again, I just loved to sing on stage and wanted to make a go of it but decided not to. Many years later I moved to Cyprus with Suzy and made my living for a year singing the pubs and hotels of Paphos. I performed as ' Big H' did an album called ' Reflections' and loved it , but reality set in and I was soon teaching again.

A few final recollections of my dad. Firstly they had a house at one time in Caerphilly. As I have mentioned before I have zero practical skills, I have never owned a tool kit, many moons since I tried to use a drill, the odd screwdriver possibly, but my theory was , get people who can do it in and do it properly, creates jobs and everyone is happy. I still follow that premise to this day. Is my lack of practical skills hereditary? Make your own mind up after this story. Mum wanted a kitchen cupboard put up to store cups etc, a simple job you may think. First hurdle was it was flatpack, these companies must employ special people and say make the instructions as difficult as possible and always leave one bit left over to make the poor person who bought this thing wonder where this bloody bit goes. It comes in 4 languages, but I might as well have read it in Serbo Croat as English as neither made any sense.

Anyway off we trotted to a DIY place, purchased said kitchen cabinet with 2, yes 2 doors and 3 shelves. What could go wrong?

A normal reasonably competent person it would be maybe an hours work, for me and dad, na. We started early , had a tea break and dinner and the thing was still not even on the wall. Dad was blaming the instructions, Mum had left the room, now dad with a drill in his hand was dangerous, he measured, put little pencil marks on the wall and stuck this pencil behind his ear thinking it made him look like a proper tradesman. He wasn't. about 6 hours later between us we got it up against the wall, the holes he had drilled in the wall were, shall we say, approximately right , we managed to get

3 of the 4 screws in and we decided that was enough. It was up (for now) and then the shelves and the doors, amazingly the 2 doors did meet in the middle and nearly shut with a push, about 8 hours later we stood back in triumph , cleaned the whole thing and told mum to get her mugs out. Pubs were just about opening and the 2 of us thought we had earned a beer.

Just as we were going to leave, we heard the smash in the kitchen and mum shouting something that was very unmum like.

What we had done is basically put the shelves in the wrong way and they were sloping downwards, so as soon as you opened the door the mugs would slide gently on to the floor. To say she was not happy was an understatement. My sister had married a great guy who was an engineer of some note and had more practical skills in his little finger than we had in our whole bodies.

By the time he came round apart from the shelves, the 3 screws had come loose and it was hanging off the wall dangling to one side. Suffice to say, Dave took about 15 minutes and the thing was perfect. Over the years Dave saved me, and my car on many occasions. I had no idea, but he would listen to it and say , the left sprocket or whatever needs replacing. The times I rang him to rescue me were many. He was a guy of infinite patience, which I never had, and he and Helen celebrate their 40th wedding anniversary in 2022. I shall be there with them. One of life's good guys.

The second of my Dad's stories was his unique way of getting rid of people when he wanted them to go. My Mum did something in the women's side of Rotary, Inner Wheel? Occasionally a bunch of women would come around the house, for a meeting/ gossip/ bitch. Dad was banished upstairs, he had a little pottering room where he wrote, read etc. When the sherries had hit these women and the noises were getting louder and louder, he had enough by then, so he would creep downstairs and in a separate room he would put a tape or record on. It would be a Welsh Choir blasting out the Welsh National Anthem, all these women would stand and sing, while Dad was opening the back door to usher them out. Absolutely brilliant, he never offended but it was so subtle. I would be in the other room , smirking to myself ,and he would always give me a knowing wink. He was an absolute bloody star.

Anyway to move on my memories of the Christmas period over the years…..

In long discussions with my sister, I sometimes forget particular Christmases as we moved so often or dad was on duty that day, the later Christmases are clearer. When I was smaller, Christmas started as soon as bonfire night finished. Trying to explain bonfire night to someone who was not British made it sound ridiculous. I remember Lily looking at me in her slightly incredulous way saying so you light a big fire about some dude who broke into the Houses of Parliament , then light what were expensive fireworks into the air for a few seconds? Yep.

Then you think to yourself how dangerous it was, bangers and jumping jacks, putting a rocket thing in a wonky milk bottle and hope it goes upward and not straight at you, waving sparklers into someone's face and standing outside in the cold whilst doing it. I have to say even then it seemed a pointless exercise, Dad would go off and buy his box of Standard Fireworks, set them off for a few minutes then wonder what the fuss was all about.

Health and Safety would have had a hissy fit, the only warning you would get was John and Val and even Shep the dog would warn us on Blue Peter to be careful.

For me it was just a benchmark for Christmas and the countdown had started…

In school we would start to make paper chains, today you seem to pay a ridiculous amount for indoor and outdoor decorations which would take up a fair amount of the national grid. These brightly coloured paper chains were often made by families then draped over the walls of the living room, holly sprigs shoved behind pictures and ornaments, the tree covered with tinsel and glass baubles which came out year after year.

We didn't ,but I recall people either making or buying these nativity scenes. The answers for Christmas always came from Blue Peter, who for its day was quite inventive and health and safety defying.

Who remembers making their Christmas advent crown from wire coat hangers, with a lit candle at each corner ?!! I tried once and like anything practical by me , it looked nothing like Blue Peter's (one of my major regrets in life was that I never got a Blue Peter badge).

If they gave them out in Uni for doing totally off the wall things my whole body would have been covered with badges…anyway back to food. I do recall my mum making Christmas puddings in the early days, but as time went on they were then kindly made by Mr Marks and Mr Spencer. Our Christmas day , especially when Dad had finished work, would start early, I remember going down to Cardiff to see Elwyn and a few beers would start then. It would get me through Christmas as for reasons I have explained I would have preferred to be in Cardiff.

I'll start with a tale from the later Christmases in my college days. On Christmas day, Mum would start cooking early, now love her , she was quite a good cook, but everything had to be cooked shall we say thoroughly and was 'well done'. Mum and Sis would be left to sort this out. Now there were strict opening times in bars and clubs of 12 till 2 on Christmas day. Me and Dad were allowed out at 12 but dinner was at 1 o'clock , not 1 minute past, not 5 minutes past but dead on 1 and god help him if he was late.

Now in those early days Dad could drink, he slowed down considerably as he got older, but when I was about 18 I used to go with him , we would be in the pub or often the British Legion Club where he liked to meet his mates. All the bar staff would know him and they would draw a beer as soon as they saw him walk in, now as soon as he had this one, they were pouring another one. Being in awe of my dad I wanted to do the same. Mistake!. In that hour Dad could have done 5 pints and I was a gibbering wreck by then. He had to carve the meat which he did without fail, whereas I could barely see the table.

Dad was not a wine drinker, but he used to buy these big bottles of cheap red and white, which may as well have been paint stripper. By then I didn't care, it tasted like nectar from the gods and it was ski Sunday again, men's downhill. We all had to wear those stupid hats from the crackers, discussion who had the leg or breast, white meat or brown but, by that time I didn't care if the bloody turkey was alive or dead.

Dinner was a blur, but we did it, then I just wanted a sleep and by this time so did Dad. We crashed out for an hour or so and having had to watch the Queen talk to her subjects first in a broadcast that was probably done in August, Dad especially would go back upstairs.

About 5 o clock Mum would start to make the turkey sandwiches with cold stuffing plus little pork pies which my dad loved and pickle and left over pudding and cake and the bloody chocolate log, again later from M&S. Table was carefully laid though , best glasses, and in the later days the hostess trolley would appear.

This triggers thoughts a few years later about Christmas at my parents. Stay with me and go forward now to say the early 80's, I had 3 children 2 were born at that time , the third followed in the mid 80's, my sister had 2 , so Christmas day was now 4 adults plus my mum and dad and 4 children all around 2 to 3. A dangerous mix …., the kids would have their stockings at their home and then to Gramps and Grandma, for another session. Paper, stockings, sellotape being thrown with gay abandon in all directions. Dad forgetting that half these toys needed batteries which he hadn't got, so kids crying because they couldn't get their bloody toys working. Mum telling Dad off for forgetting them .The routine would generally be the same as maybe 10 years previously, to the pub now about 100 yards away for 12 midday , back for 1. Maybe now my brother in law as well. As ever damage would be done and the 100 yards home would now be about 3 miles before I weaved my way to the front door. Routine as always was Dad cut the turkey, but with 4 kids as well, it wasn't as well controlled as before. In the intervening years his wine selection hadn't really improved. Still cheap red and white wine, from the bottom budget shelf for the poor and alcoholics in Victoria wine etc by which time I was bladdered. I was living in Cardiff at the time, and sometimes I wasn't allowed to drive home The day would be chaos, and would drive my dear old mum, who liked things in their place, to distraction. Now my dear Sister Helen is 6 years younger than me, but about 10 years wiser and about 20 years more sensible. She had all the calm and sensible genes and I had none, and meant I would make endless wrong, spur of the moment, decisions .

Dad as he got older, needed his afternoon sleep even more, now he loved his grandchildren with everything he had, but 4 kids crawling all over him at about 3 o clock when he wanted to sleep was not his best time. If we were going back to Cardiff, he would call me over and whisper 'it's been great having you but it's time for you to bugger off home'…point taken.

My sister was more use anyway as she would be sorting out the kitchen with my mum, in her calm unflustered way. I now decided it was time for a walk, they lived in a village with a disused quarry close by, so off I would stroll, no light, difficult to find your way on a balmy Welsh December evening. Dangerous old paths and I would normally either fall, trip, stay there and fall asleep, then wake up wondering where the hell I was. Eventually remembering and trying to get back, usually with blood coming from somewhere. People were then half asleep at home and those who were awake didn't look surprised as they thought I was upstairs. Then I would sit down with the Morecombe and Wise Christmas show and be the only person on the planet who would eat a whole packet of figs in one sitting ,before starting on the Cadburys Roses, and eating all the favourites, especially the caramel ones, so all that was left were the crap coffee and strawberry ones that nobody wanted.

How I would love another one of those days again......

Hang on, and stay with me as I go back to my childhood days now. In those days the excitement was palpable, stockings or sacks were double checked and ready to be put at the end of our beds, and sleep was almost impossible on Christmas eve. We must have and there were full stockings at the end of the bed. The bottom always had a Satsuma and coin, chocolate money, selection boxes , puzzle books, small toys, colouring books , a packet of pens , the Beano or Dandy, but for me it was the Victor, with the fearless Alf Tupper, 'The Tough of the Track who thrilled boys for many years. He was a welder who lived on a diet of fish and chips. A true hero.Apart from these we had a main present. The only one I remember is a Meccano set, which to a non practical boy, didn't last long, a chemistry set which again didn't rock my boat but the thought and effort was always there. Me and Helen have often talked about the fact that neither of us ever had a bike as a present I never knew why and to this day I have never ever ridden a bike ......My sister was telling me only recently that she had a bucket list and on that list was to learn to ride a bike .She was chuffed that she now had a certificate for cycling proficiency!!

I had no bucket list then, the only thing that was added later was I wanted to write a book, hence this effort. I have never been camping, someone tell me what the attraction is of sleeping on wet grass, with a loo about a mile away and there would inevitably be a decent hotel close by? I have also never ridden a bike, never been skiing never been on a horse, never had a tattoo and I feel I have not really missed anything. It was a different world in the 50's and 60's and my recollections are confused by the fact that we spent it in so many different houses, but through our whole life Helen and I wanted for nothing...

School days are a similar blur . In the 50's and 60's there were no state preschools or nurseries, so for most children turning 5 the first day of starting school was the first day they had left their parents. Most mothers then did not work so it was the first time this bond had been broken.

I recall visits from the school nurse, especially the nit nurse who would examine every child for headlice, and if you had it the cleaning and scrubbing was horrendous. I had the polio vaccine on a lump of sugar. I recall that classes were very big due to 'baby boomers' born after WW2. Just one teacher meant discipline was tight and teachers were not averse to a rap on the knuckles or worse if needs be.

Teaching was ' chalk and talk' and basically rote learning. On the one hand mums were trying to open minds and create an enquiring mind then ,bam , as long as the 3 R's were drummed into you, reading , writing and arithmetic it was deemed OK, but it wasn't good enough for an enquiring mind like mine who was always asking Why? Or What? to the annoyance of many teachers. Just copy it down even if you had no idea what it meant. It was only when I got to the 6th form in Sandfields that this enquiring mind was allowed to develop, and ever since those days I have encouraged all my own students over the years to argue, debate and look at different views .Today with the internet, knowledge is easy, applying that knowledge is the key.

Anyway off that hobby horse, throughout the UK there was a strong sense of being British. My parents were staunch royalists and even from an early age I was not, but it wasn't worth an argument at home. In Wales thankfully it concentrated on our country and that is why St David's day was a big occasion. Mum making sure we all wore daffodils to school in our Welsh costumes and the St David's day concert in the morning which all parents came to see and then joy of joys, the afternoon off school.

As I got older those days instilled a feeling of nationalism and love of the Country which is still there today. I have not lived in Wales for many years- Lived in many other parts of the UK, Cyprus and now Spain. But that love of being born Welsh is still with me as I am sure it is the same with many of you. My mum gave me a little poster when I was going to Cyprus to live saying ' To be born Welsh is not being born with a silver spoon in your mouth, but music in your heart and passion in your soul' Nothing has changed....

Dear readers, my initial journey ends here, I have summed up my thoughts in my final pages .I could have written much more but I wanted to pass on the essence of growing up in those times through my eyes. It is for you to judge. I hope it triggers your own thoughts, nostalgia is a powerful emotion and writing this book certainly triggered mine.

For good or bad I am pleased and proud that I actually did it.

CHAPTER 22

AND FINALLY..

Having taken 30 years to put this book together, I need to consider what I have learnt from the experience.

It has triggered emotions in me which I thought were dead and buried, and as one memory came to mind, it tended to trigger off others and then it is was like a chain reaction.

I have had no training in how to write, not sure if that is a good or bad thing. For me it has meant I have had to write from my heart and let my emotions take over. It has triggered thoughts which even as I was writing have made me smile. Sometimes wistfully . Sometimes chuckle out loud. Sometimes sad and reflective. Sometimes it brings a tear to my eye which I can brush away. Sometimes I have to stop to really cry. Sometimes it makes me angry at mistakes and decisions I have made. Sometimes regret that I should or shouldn't have done the things that I did.

I realise that life is a series of 'what if's' and if you had rolled the dice and another number had come up, your life would have gone in another direction . I imagine it is the same for all of us.

When we make those decisions we have to make the best of it, good or bad. If you make a wrong decision so be it, you made that decision, it's no one else's fault.

In my 69 years on this planet I have met 1000's of people, many just flit into your life briefly and you never remember them, others stay longer and some will stay in your head forever, even if you don't see them again. Others become part of your DNA and are just part of your life until you take your last breath.

I have been blessed in the fact that most people I have come into contact with are good people and during my life, including the people I have tried to articulate in this book , have added to the richness of my life . For that I thank all those people and many others from the bottom of my heart. I have mentioned often that life is a series of jigsaw pieces. For all of us, that jigsaw is never completed, but enjoy the life you have ,and just keep adding another piece of the jigsaw every day .

I initially decided to write this book for me and me alone, but it became also for my mum and dad, but if it has hit a chord or released a memory in others that is an additional bonus.

All of you who read this , I hope you get some enjoyment from it, it has been a labour of love for me, so enjoy it before it ends up in the bargain bucket in WH Smiths!!

Stay safe and have a happy and peaceful life.

Howard xx